steven holl

Herausgegeben von Edited by
LIUBISA – Familien-Privatstiftung

Texte von Texts by
Gudrun Hausegger
Othmar Pruckner
Dietmar Steiner

world of wine
LOISIUM

HATJE
CANTZ

Herausgeber Editor LIUBISA – Familien-Privatstiftung

Konzept und Redaktion Concept and Editing Gudrun Hausegger

Lektorat Copyediting Claudia Mazanek

Übersetzungen Translations

Deutsch Englisch German English Kimberly Callecod-Weinrich,
Roderick O'Donovan, Peter Waugh

Englisch Deutsch English German Thomas Rath

Visualisierungskonzept und Gestaltung Design Gabriele Lenz

Mitarbeit Assistants Ewa Kaja, Elmar Bertsch

Schrift Typeface

Univers von Adrian Frutiger (1957)

Zapf Renaissance Antiqua von Hermann Zapf (1987)

Papier Paper Luxosamt, 150 g/m²

Druck Printing Dr. Cantz'sche Druckerei, Ostfildern

Buchbinderei Binding Conzella Verlagsbuchbinderei, Urban Meister GmbH,
Aschheim-Dornach

Fotonachweis Photo credits Architekturzentrum Wien 50–51
Florian Burger 92–94 Foto LOISIUM 9 Andreas Gattermann 92–93
Robert Herbst 15, 54–55, 78, 86–87, 93, 97, 110 Hertha Hurnaus 39–40,
57, 62–64, 79, 97 ko a la 111 Steven Holl Architects 40, 78, 108
Kamptal/Andreas Hofer 14–15, 20 Patti McConville/TIPS/picturedesk.com 21
Zita Oberwalder 50–51 Christian Richters 60 Sam/Ott-Reinisch 94–97, 109
Margherita Spiluttini Umschlagabbildung Cover illustration, 4–5, 38, 41,
45–47, 58–59, 61, 65–71, 102–103

Erschienen im Published by Hatje Cantz Verlag, Zeppelinstraße 32
73760 Ostfildern Deutschland Germany, Tel. +49 711 4405-200
Fax +49 711 4405-220, www.hatjecantz.com

Hatje Cantz books are available internationally at selected bookstores and
from the following distribution partners:
USA – D.A.P., Distributed Art Publishers, New York www.artbook.com
UK – Art Books International, London www.art-bks.com
Australia – Tower Books, Frenchs Forest (Sydney) www.towerbooks.com.au
France – Interart, Paris www.interart.fr
Belgium – Exhibitions International, Leuven www.exhibitionsinternational.be
Switzerland – Scheidegger, Affoltern am Albis www.ava.ch
For Asia, Japan, South America, and Africa, as well as for general questions,
please contact Hatje Cantz directly at sales@hatjecantz.de, or visit our
homepage www.hatjecantz.com for further information.

ISBN 978-3-7757-1949-0

Printed in Germany

Inhalt
Contents

Othmar Pruckner

Das LOISIUM steht nicht im Niemandsland und auch nicht für sich allein. Die Dreiheit aus silberglänzendem Kubus, unterirdischer Weinkeller-Erlebniswelt und schickem Designer-Hotel befindet sich in einer der faszinierendsten Kulturlandschaften Österreichs, mitten im Weinbaugebiet des östlichen Flachlands, rund siebzig Kilometer von der Bundeshauptstadt Wien entfernt. In der kurzen Zeit seiner Existenz – die Eröffnung fand im September 2003 statt – hat das spektakuläre Bauwerk des amerikanischen Architekten Steven Holl bereits viel Aufsehen erregt, Bilder davon sind längst um die ganze Welt gegangen. Bevor im Weiteren die Geschichte des Projekts dokumentiert wird, bevor Idee wie Details sorgfältig beschrieben werden, soll das Umfeld, in dem es überhaupt wachsen und gedeihen konnte, kurz skizziert werden.

Zu allererst: Das LOISIUM ist ein Zeichen dafür, dass im kleinen Österreich seit einiger Zeit großer Wein gekeltert wird. Es ist ein Symbol für die tausendjährige Geschichte des Weinbaus in der Region und demonstriert, fernab von jedem museal-volkskundlichen Zugang, das Selbstbewusstsein eines neu erstarkten, dynamischen Wirtschaftszweigs. Das LOISIUM als Eventzentrum und Erlebniswelt neuen Zuschnitts spiegelt aber auch das große Interesse der Österreicherinnen und Österreicher an dieser alten Kulturpflanze, an diesem jahrtausendealten, hymnisch gepriesenen und manchmal auch verteufelten Getränk.

Das LOISIUM, sagen manche, sei eine Anmaßung. Es verlangt ja lautstark nach höchster internationaler Aufmerksamkeit, obwohl Österreich, jetzt einmal aus

The LOISIUM does not stand in a no-man's land, and it does not stand alone. The triumvirate of gleaming silver cube, underground wine cellar world, and chic designer hotel is located in one of the most fascinating cultural landscapes of Austria, in the middle of the winegrowing area of the eastern plains, about seventy kilometers from the capital Vienna. In the short span of its existence—the opening took place in September 2003—the spectacular building of the American architect Steven Holl has already caused quite a stir, and images of it have made their way across the globe. Before the history of the project is documented, and before the idea as well as the details can be described meticulously, the environment in which it could grow and flourish should be sketched briefly.

First and foremost: the LOISIUM is the sign that in little Austria great wines are being pressed, and this for some time now. It is a symbol for the thousand-year-old history of viticulture in the region and demonstrates, far beyond any museum-like folkloric approach, the assertiveness of a newly vitalized, dynamic economic sector. The LOISIUM is a new type of event center and theme park yet as such reflects the huge interest Austrians have in this ancient crop, in this millennial-old, alternately praised and demonized drink.

The LOISIUM, some say, is presumptuous. It clamours loudly for intense international attention even though Austria, seen from a global perspective, is no more than a wine dwarf. Up until now, this country has been known in the wide world primarily for its musicians and skiing champions and less for its superb vintners.

Vorige Doppelseite: Blick auf Langenlois mit Besucherzentrum und Hotel im Hintergrund
Previous pages: View of Langenlois, showing the visitors' center and the hotel in the background

globaler Perspektive gesehen, ja nichts anderes als ein Wein-Zwerg ist. Das Land war in der weiten Welt bislang vorwiegend für seine Musiker und Skifahrer-Kaiser bekannt und weniger für seine grandiosen Winzerkönige; zu den geschätzten 280 Millionen Hektolitern Welt-Jahresproduktion an Wein trägt das Land der hohen Berge und der schönen Seen gerade einmal runde 2,3 Millionen Hektoliter bei – weniger als ein Prozent, eine vernachlässigbare Größe. Der Tempel des modernen Weinbaus, so könnte man kritisieren, hätte wohl zu Frankreich, Spanien oder Italien gepasst, aber doch nicht ins alpine Binnenland Österreich. Doch alles hat seinen guten Grund: In Österreich hat sich nämlich in den letzten zwei Jahrzehnten ein echtes Wein-Wunder ereignet. Nach einem bösen ‚Weinskandal‘ im Jahr 1985 wurde die Produktion landauf, landab deutlich zurückgefahren, die Winzer setzten statt auf Quantität auf Qualität. Naturnahe Techniken hielten im einst chemielastigen Weinbau Einzug; die Trauben wurden nun äußerst vorsichtig gelesen und, gehätschelt wie Trüffelknollen, statt in riesigen Maischbottichen in kleinen Steigen zur Traubenpresse gebracht. Revolutionär denkende Söhne zeigten ihren Vätern, wie man ganz gewöhnlichen Most zu wertvollem Wein vergolden konnte. Österreichs Weine sind heute absolut ‚trendy‘ – namentlich der Grüne Veltliner konnte sich als typisch österreichischer Weißer sogar in Übersee einen guten Namen machen. Ob in den *New York Times* oder im *Wine Spectator*, überall werden die heimischen Produkte hymnisch rezensiert, heimsen Österreichs Winzer Preise im Dutzendpack ein.

Of the estimated 280 million hectoliters of wine produced around the world each year, the country of the high mountains and gorgeous lakes contributes a meagre 2.3 million hectolitres—less than one percent, a negligible contribution. A temple of modern viticulture, one could protest, would have been a natural fit in France, Spain or Italy, but hardly in alpine, land-locked Austria.
Yet there is a reason for everything. In the past two decades, a veritable wine *wunder* has come to pass in Austria. Following the infamous 'wine scandal' of 1985, production was reduced significantly across the entire country. The vintners began to concentrate on quality instead of quantity. Near-natural viticultural techniques came into play where previously chemicals had dominated. Now, grapes were selected with the utmost of care and, fondled like fine truffles, brought to the grape press in small fruit crates instead of enormous mashing vats. Sons with revolutionary ideas showed their fathers how common must could be turned into precious wine. And today, Austria's wines are utterly trendy: as a typical Austrian white, the *Grüner Veltliner* has literally been able to make a name for itself, even abroad. Whether in The *New York Times* or in *Wine Spectator*, native products have been receiving rave reviews everywhere and Austria's vintners have been raking in prizes by the dozen.
The great majority of Austria's wines grow in the flatter, warmer eastern half of the country. The best red wines prosper in Burgenland, on the border to Hungary. Above all the *Blaufränkische*, an indigenous wine variety, has received

Österreichs Weine wachsen zum überwiegenden Teil in der flacheren, wärmeren Osthälfte des Landes. An der Grenze zu Ungarn, im Burgenland, gedeihen die besten Rotweine. Vor allem der Blaufränkische erhält als autochthone Weinsorte internationale Anerkennung. Die Süßweine, die um den Neusiedler See produziert werden, sind unangefochten Weltspitze, daneben haben es auch die Rieslinge aus der niederösterreichischen Wachau zu großem Ruhm gebracht. An steilen Hängen, gestützt von tausenden Steinterrassen, wird hier seit Jahrhunderten in mühevoller Handarbeit vor allem Urgesteinsriesling angebaut.

Die mit Abstand weitest verbreitete Rebsorte ist aber der bereits genannte Grüne Veltliner; die Sorte macht sich auf mehr als einem Drittel der gesamten Wein-gartenfläche Österreichs breit. Im Weinviertel – dem fruchtbaren, welligen Hügel-land, das sich malerisch zwischen Wien und der slowakischen bzw. tschechischen Grenze erstreckt, ist er der absolute Herr im Land. Ebenso im Kamptal, einem kleinen, eigenständigen Weinbaugebiet mitten in Niederösterreich, nördlich der Donau, nahe der Wachau. Der Kamp, zur näheren Erklärung, ist ein romantisches Flüsschen, das aus dem Mittelgebirge des Waldviertels in hunderten Schlingen und Mäandern zur Donau hinstrebt. In seinem Unterlauf, dort, wo das Tal flach und breit wird und sich die mächtige Donau schon erahnen lässt, wird seit vielen hunderten Jahren Wein angebaut und mit Wein gehandelt.

Das Zentrum dieses alten Weinbaugebiets ist Langenlois, von seinen Bewohnern auch liebevoll ‚Lois' genannt. Am Rand dieser kleinen, etwas mehr als

international acclaim. The sweet wines which are produced around the Neusiedler See area are indisputably world class. In addition to these, *Riesling* varieties from the Lower Austrian Wachau have experienced great glory. For centuries, the *Urgesteinriesling* type in particular has been cultivated painstakingly by hand on steep slopes which are buttressed by thousands of stone terraces.

However, the by far most common grape variety is the above-mentioned *Grüner Veltliner*; this variety has made itself at home in more than a third of the total winegrowing area in Austria. In the Weinviertel—with its fecund rolling hills stretching picturesquely from Vienna to the Slovakian and Czech borders—the *Grüner Veltliner* rules the roost. It also dominates in the Kamptal, or Kamp Valley, a small autonomous viticultural area in the middle of Lower Austria, north of the Danube, near the Wachau. The Kamp, by way of explanation, is a romantic creek who from its source in the low mountain ranges of the Waldviertel loops and meanders until it reaches the Danube. In its lower reaches, where the valley becomes flat and broad and where the powerful Danube can begin to be divined, wine has been cultivated and traded for many hundreds of years.

The center of this ancient viticultural area is Langenlois, affectionately dubbed 'Lois' by its residents. On the outskirts of this small city with just over 7,000 inhabitants, Steven Holl was able to build his LOISIUM; thus the question of the rather peculiar-sounding name of the object has now answered itself. Langenlois and the LOISIUM are markers for the absolute hot spot of Austrian

Rechts: Luftaufnahme Langenlois: Zentrum mit Pfarr-kirche und Kornplatz

Right: Aerial view of Langenlois: town center showing parish church and Kornplatz

siebentausend Einwohner zählenden Stadt konnte Steven Holl sein LOISIUM errichten; die Frage nach dem eigentümlich klingenden Namen des Objekts beantwortet sich nun von selbst.

Langenlois und das LOISIUM markieren also einen absoluten ‚Hot Spot' des österreichischen Weinbaus – und das mit gutem Grund: Langenlois ist eine der trockensten Städte Österreichs. Die Sommer sind heiß, die warme Luft strömt aus dem pannonischen Osten bis hierher. In den Nächten aber fließt auch in der warmen Jahreszeit kühle Luft aus dem höher gelegenen Waldviertel ins Tal – ein Kleinklima, das gerade den Grünen Veltliner besonders fruchtig, würzig, frisch und ‚pfeffrig' macht. Dazu bringen Kamp und Donau ausreichend hohe Luftfeuchtigkeit. Der Sommer dauert im Kamptal lang, der Herbst ist so mild, dass in den letzten Jahren die Trauben bis weit in den November hinein gelesen werden konnten. Zu allem Überfluss stehen große Teile der Kamptaler Weingärten auf fruchtbarem Löss; in das hellgelbe, weiche Material ließen sich auch wunderbar tiefe Kellerröhren graben. Die Winzer fahren in engen, steilen Lössgräben zu ihren Weingärten, hinaus ins Steinmaßl oder zum Dechant, zur Weinträgerin oder auf den Geißberg, ins Vögerl oder auf den Heiligenstein: Jede Lage, jede Riede hat ihre spezifischen Eigenheiten, ihre besonderen Qualitäten.

Die Gegend rund um das lang gezogene Städchen ist überhaupt extrem vielgestaltig. Steile, terrassierte Hänge und weite, flache Felder, kleine Tälchen, schattige Wälder, grüne Wiesen, wogende Felder, Donauschotter und Urgestein,

viticulture. There could not be a better place for the flourishing of grapevines. Langenlois is one of the driest cities in Austria. The summers are hot; warm air flows here all the way from the Pannonian east. Yet at night, cool air from higher elevations in the Waldviertel flows, even in the warmer seasons, into the valley—a microclimate which makes the *Grüner Veltliner* in particular especially fruity, spicy, fresh and 'peppery.' As well, the Kamp and the Danube provide for sufficiently high air humidity. Summers are long in the Kamp Valley and autumns are so mild that in the past few years, grapes were able to be selected even into late November. To top it off, large portions of the Kamp Valley vineyards stand on fertile loess; the pale yellow, soft material lends itself well to the digging of wonderfully deep cellar tunnels. The vintners go to their vineyards by way of narrow, steep loess trenches, out to the Steinmassl or to Dechant; to the Weinträgerin or up on the Geissberg; in Vögerl or on the Heiligenstein: every location and every plot has its specific character and special qualities.

The area surrounding the elongated village is in fact extremely diverse. Steep terraced slopes and broad flat expanses; small valleys, shady forests, green meadows and undulant fields; Danubian and prehistoric rock; loess and alluvial land—in a highly dense space all these things may be faund next to and on top of each other. This marvellous natural diversity also makes the wines of the region extremely varied and attracts wine aficionados from every region of the globe. The culture of fine wine has made itself at home; the art of wine tasting

Löss und Schwemmland, alles ist hier auf engstem Raum neben- und auch durcheinander zu finden. Diese wunderbare natürliche Vielfalt macht die Weine der Region so extrem abwechslungsreich und zieht Weinfreunde aus allen Weltgegenden hierher. – Die Feinweinkultur hat Einzug gehalten und somit ist die Kunst des Weinkostens auch in Langenlois zu so etwas wie einem neuen Volkssport geworden. Sorten, Jahrgänge und auch Rieden wollen ,erkostet' werden, nicht nur im Gourmetlokal, sondern auch am Heurigentisch wird gefachsimpelt, dass sich die Fassdauben biegen. Zum Trost für alle, die da nicht mitkönnen: Es sollen auch schon ausgewiesene Experten daran gescheitert sein, einen Grünen Veltliner von einem Weißburgunder zu unterscheiden.

Viele Weinreisende suchen die Nähe der Winzer. Die Fans von Bründlmayer, Jurtschitsch, Loimer oder Steininger wollen ihren neuen Idolen, den Halbgöttern der Steinterrassen und Hanglagen die Reverenz erweisen. Sie wollen deren Schatzkammern, die Weinkeller, mit eigenen Augen sehen, wollen die letzten Geheimnisse der weit verzweigten Kellerröhren ergründen und unbedingt einen seltenen, ,eigentlich' nicht mehr lieferbaren Jahrgang doch noch ergattern. Bei der alljährlich wiederkehrenden ,Tour de Vin', einem Wochenende, an dem führende Winzer der Wachau und des Kamptals Tage der Offenen Tür veranstalten, werden diese prominenten Leitbetriebe mit schöner Regelmässigkeit überrannt. Die neuen Weinheiligen ertragen den Rummel freilich mit großer Gelassenheit, denn Weinfreunde sind ein gebildetes, treues und last but not least zahlungskräftiges Publikum.

has always been something of a national sport, also in Langenlois. Varieties, vintages and even different plots must be tasted and explored. At both gourmet restaurants and on *Heuriger* benches, wine terminology is tossed around with enough vigour to bend the staves of the casks. But to comfort all those who cannot keep up with the technicalities: even proven experts have been known to fail in the attempt to tell a *Grüner Veltliner* from a *Weissburgunder*.

Many wine tourists seek above all proximity to the vintners. Fans of Bründlmayer, Jurtschitsch, Loimer or Steininger wish to pay their respects to the new idols, the demigods of the stone terraces and slopes. They want to see the treasure chambers—the wine cellars—with their own eyes; they want to feel out the last mysteries of the vast intertwined cellar tunnels. They wish to get hold of by any means necessary the rare vintage which is supposedly no longer available. At the annual 'Tour de Vin,' a weekend on which leading vintners of the Wachau and Kamp Valley organize open houses, these prominent leading winemakers find their cellars practically stormed with assuring regularity. These new wine gods bear the fuss with great aplomb, as after all wine aficionados are an educated, loyal and, last but not least, affluent audience.

Wine from Langenlois is fashionable again, yet wine has been here for practically forever. Wine, says sociologist Reinhold Knoll, is the civilizing root of this city. Let us take a brief look to the past. At the very latest, it was the Romans who brought vine stocks to the Danube. During the era of mass migration most

Langenloiser Wein ist wieder in Mode, doch Wein gibt es hier schon seit beinahe ewigen Zeiten. Der Wein, so sagt der Soziologe Reinhold Knoll, ist die zivilisatorische Wurzel dieser Stadt. Schauen wir also kurz zurück: Spätestens die Römer brachten die Weinstöcke an die Donau. In der Völkerwanderungszeit verschwanden die meisten Weinkulturen in der Region zwar wieder, ab dem 9. Jahrhundert aber führten Mönche die alte Kulturpflanze dann neuerlich und dauerhaft ein. Angeblich war im Mittelalter die mit Wein bepflanzte Fläche zehnmal so groß wie heute – der Hektarertrag freilich dramatisch geringer und die Zahl der Ernte-Totalausfälle deutlich höher.

Der Ort Langenlois wurde um das Jahr 1100 planmäßig angelegt. Salz, Holz- und nicht zuletzt Weinhandel brachten bald Geld in die Gegend und wie in vielen anderen Märkten und Kleinstädten Niederösterreichs ließen sich auch hier mehrere jüdische Händlerfamilien nieder.

Als besonders wichtig für die Geschichte des Weinbaus gilt das Jahr 1784. Kaiser Josef II. gewährte den Weinhauern das ‚Ausschankrecht‘ – seit dem Mittelalter bestehende Weinschenken wurden somit von Gesetzes wegen anerkannt und leben bis heute als allseits beliebte Heurigenlokale fort. Nach einer Hochblüte im 18. Jahrhundert zwang in der zweiten Hälfte des 19. Jahrhunderts eine lange andauernde Kälteperiode zur Aufgabe höher gelegener Weingärten. Und danach kam die größte Katastrophe überhaupt: Die aus den USA eingeschleppte Reblaus vernichtete einen Großteil der Weinkulturen. Erst als man begann, die edlen

viticulture in the region disappeared anew, but starting with the nineth century, monks reintroduced the ancient crop and established it permanently. Supposedly, the total area which was covered by vineyards was ten times as large during the Middle Ages as it is today, whereby the yield per hectare was dramatically lower and the incidence of total loss of harvest much higher.

The site of Langenlois was methodically laid out in the year 1100. Salt, timber and also wine trading brought money to the area and as in many other markets and small cities in Lower Austria, several Jewish merchant families also settled here.

The year 1784 was especially important in the history of viticulture. Emperor Joseph II granted winegrowers the *Ausschankrecht*, or right to sell alcohol, thereby officially recognizing the wine inns which had existed since the Middle Ages and live on until today in the form of the universally popular *Heuriger* establishments. Following a zenith in the eighteenth century, a prolonged cold spell in the second half of the nineteenth century forced the abandonment of vineyards at higher elevations. And then came the biggest catastrophe of all: phylloxera, inadvertently introduced from the U.S.A., destroyed the bulk of viticulture. Only after growers began to graft the grapes on pest-resistant rootstocks was the survival of the wine industry certain.

It is hard to imagine Langenlois without wine. The juice of the grape, wine, has always been an export product for which handsome sums would be paid. Wine meant adequate occupational opportunities for craftsmen, hauliers, merchants

Reben auf schädlingsresistente Trägerstöcke aufzupfropfen, war der Fortbestand der Weinwirtschaft gesichert.

Ohne Wein ist Langenlois kaum vorstellbar. Der Rebensaft, der Wein, war immer ein ‚Exportgut', mit dem man gute Preise erzielen konnte. Er bot einer Vielzahl von Handwerkern, Fuhrwerkern, Händlern, aber auch Taglöhnern und Erntearbeitern hinreichend Erwerbsmöglichkeiten. Die Kulturen veränderten seit dem Frühmittelalter nicht nur das Landschaftsbild nachhaltig; auch in der Stadt, in den Hausfassaden spiegelte sich sichtbar der Wohlstand.

Fast jede Familie besaß irgendwo wenigstens ein kleines Stück Weingarten und zwar bis weit ins 20. Jahrhundert hinein. 1976 gab es in der Stadt noch über tausend (!) Weinbaubetriebe, 2006 allerdings nur mehr fünfhundert. In nur dreißig Jahren halbierte sich die Zahl der Winzer: so etwas nennt man in der Fachsprache trocken ‚Strukturwandel'. Viele der kleinen Weinhauer konnten einfach nicht mithalten, viele Nebenerwerbsbauern hörten damit auf, Trauben zu pressen und den Wein in Flaschen zu füllen. Das mag man bedauern, doch noch immer ist die Kamptaler ebenso wie die gesamte Österreichische Weinwirtschaft kleinteilig genug. Die durchschnittliche Betriebsgröße liegt bei eineinhalb Hektar, wobei es erst bei fünf Hektar ökonomisch halbwegs Sinn macht, einen Betrieb im Vollerwerb zu führen.

Die andere Seite der Medaille ist die erfreulichere: Viele junge Winzer sind sehr rasch sehr populär geworden. Gefeiert wie Popstars schmücken sie sich und ihre

but also day laborers and harvesters. Since the Early Middle Ages, this crop has changed not only the landscape in a sustained manner, but also the city, whose house façades radiated affluence.

Almost every family owned at least a small piece of a vineyard; this was the case up until far into the twentieth century. In 1976, there were still over a thousand (!) winegrowing operations, but by 2006 this number was down to five hundred. In only thirty years, the number of vintners had been halved, a phenomenon euphemistically called 'structural transformation.' Many of the small winegrowers could simply not keep up, and many who farmed on a sideline basis ceased pressing grapes and filling wine into bottles. This may be regrettable, yet like the Austrian wine industry as a whole, the Kamp Valley industry is still fragmented enough. The average size of operations is one and a half hectares, whereby it only becomes financially viable to engage in viticulture as a full-time occupation with five hectares or more.

The other side of the coin is more gratifying. Many young vintners have become very popular very quickly. Celebrated like pop stars, they often crown themselves and their operations with modern architecture. They have the labels of their wine bottles designed by famous native artists. And they have managed—in the Kamp Valley as well—to kindle a new cult surrounding the ancient crop. At the same time, their success means that many of the other remaining 'little guys' can live well, if only as grape suppliers.

Weinlese
Wine harvest

Weinlese
Wine harvest

Kellergassen
Wine cellar lanes

Kellergassenfest
Festival in the wine cellar lanes

Betriebe gern mit neuer Architektur, lassen sie die Etiketten ihrer Weinflaschen von berühmten heimischen Künstlern entwerfen. Sie haben es – auch im Kamptal – geschafft, einen neuen Kult um die alte Kulturpflanze zur entfachen. Und gleichzeitig lässt ihr Erfolg auch etliche der übrig gebliebenen ‚Kleinen' gut leben, und sei es als Traubenlieferanten.

Quereinsteiger versuchen sich erfolgreich als Weinproduzenten. Neue Weinlokale werden eröffnet, die Vinotheken gestürmt. Wobei dem ‚Heurigen' – der klassischen Weinschänke – noch immer eine besondere Rolle zufällt. Ob beim Kellerfest, im Nobel- oder im einfachen Winzerheurigen: Hier wird gelebt, gelacht, geredet. Hier existiert auch noch so etwas wie eine selbstverständliche Nähe zwischen unterschiedlichen sozialen Schichten und Generationen. Wer gern darüber klagt, dass im Zeitalter der medialen Überflutung die zwischenmenschliche Kommunikation nur mehr in Rudimenten existiere, dem sei geraten, an einem lauen Sommerwochenende in die Zöbinger Kellergasse, auf den Langenloiser Sauberg oder in eines der vielen anderen Heurigenlokale der Umgebung zu pilgern. Dem sei – neben dem Besuch des LOISIUMs – vor allem empfohlen, eines der vielen Kellergassenfeste zu besuchen. Grammelschmalzbrot und Winzerjause, dazu ein, zwei oder auch drei ‚G'spritzte' haben schon aus manch hartnäckigem Misanthropen einen glückseligen Menschen gemacht – wenigstens für einige Stunden. Klar ist dabei: In jedem Fall sollte das Credo des seligen Erzkomödianten Hans Moser Beachtung finden. ‚Wenn ich mein Weinderl beiß', dann ist mir

Newcomers to the branch have been able to chalk up success as wine producers. New wine bars are being opened and the local vinotheques are being stormed. Yet the *Heuriger*—the traditional wine inn—continues to assume a special role. Whether at a cellar festival, at a fancy or a rustic vintner's *Heuriger*: there is laughter, dialogue and life. And here there is even something approaching a natural nearness among different social classes and generations. Those who complain about the lack of interpersonal communication in an age of media overkill should pay a visit on a mild summer weekend to the Zöbinger cellar lane, the Sauberg in Langenlois, or to any of the many *Heuriger* inns of the area. And in addition to a visit to the LOISIUM, it is highly recommended that they visit one of the many cellar lane festivals. Typical fare such as *Grammelschmalzbrot* (dark rye bread spread with a specific type of lard) and other vintner snacks, imbibed with two or perhaps three *G'spritzte*, have turned many a stubborn misanthrope into a beatific mensch—at least for a few hours.

In any case, the credo of the deceased Austrian comedian Hans Moser should be heeded: 'Wenn ich mein Weinderl beiß,' dann ist mir wurscht der Preis, ich trink vom besten, aber zizerlweis.' (Keeping his unique mumbled delivery in mind, the rough translation runs along the lines of, 'When I drink my wine it is with pleasure, and I don't care what the price is; I drink the best, but do it slowly.') Fifty years later, his words still reflect an entirely appropriate attitude to the consumption of wine.

wurscht der Preis, ich trink vom besten, aber zizerlweis' – nuschelte er unverwechselbar und hat damit schon vor fünfzig Jahren die einzig richtige Einstellung zum Weinkonsum gepredigt.

Das Kamptal, um wieder ins geographische Fach zu wechseln, war schon in der Zeit der Monarchie als ‚Sommerfrische' beliebt. Nach einer großen Stille in der Zeit des Wirtschaftswunders der 1970er und 1980er Jahre erlebt die Region zur Zeit eine bemerkenswerte Renaissance. Neben der unverbrauchten Naturlandschaft des Wald- und Weinviertels, neben der Stille der unverbauten Kampufer sind es zahlreiche Kulturdenkmäler und Kunstschätze, die das Weinland rund um Langenlois interessant für Ausflüge und Kurzurlaube machen. Das pittoreske Schloss Grafenegg, nur sechs Kilometer von Langenlois entfernt, wird soeben zum niederösterreichischen Festspielzentrum aus- und umgebaut. Die Stadt Krems, an der nahen Donau gelegen, ist ein städtebauliches Juwel mit mittelalterlichem Flair. Stift Göttweig, Dürnstein, die malerischen Orte der Wachau sind in kurzer Fahrzeit zu erreichen. Keine zwanzig Kilometer kampaufwärts von Langenlois liegt die bekannte Sommerfrische Gars mit seiner Babenbergerburg, fünf Kilometer weiter thront hoch über dem Kamptal die Rosenburg, ein österreichisches Wahrzeichen.

Das Barockjuwel Stift Altenburg ist keine dreißig Minuten entfernt. Dort wurde, wie an etlichen anderen Orten der Region, ein prachtvoller Schaugarten angelegt; der ‚Gartenkunst' wird seit einem erfolgreichen ‚Gartenfestival' im Land ringsum

To return to geography: even in the days of the monarchy, the Kamp Valley was popular as a summer holiday destination. Following a period of calm during the *Wirtschaftswunder* of the 1970s and 1980s, the region is now experiencing a remarkable renaissance. Besides the pristine natural landscape of the Waldviertel and the Weinviertel and the silence of the unspoilt Kamp banks, it is the numerous cultural monuments and art treasures which make the wine country around Langenlois particularly interesting for excursions and weekend holidays. The picturesque Grafenegg Castle, only six kilometers from Langenlois, is currently being renovated and expanded to become Lower Austria's music festival center. The city of Krems, which lies on the nearby Danube, is a gem of city planning with Middle-Age flair. Göttweig Abbey, Dürnstein and the quaint towns of the Wachau region are within a short distance. Only twenty kilometers up the Kamp from Langenlois is the famous summer holiday resort Gars with its Babenberger Castle; five kilometers further, the Rosenburg, an Austrian landmark, is enthroned high above the Kamp Valley.

The Baroque treasure Altenburg Abbey is but thirty minutes away. There, as in many other areas of the region, magnificent show gardens have been created. Since a garden festival was crowned with success, garden art has become important all around the region. Many castles such as Mühlbach and Wiedendorf have devoted themselves to new ideas in garden design; the Arche Noah at Schiltern Castle has long been a place of pilgrimage for lovers of natural gardens.

hoher Stellenwert beigemessen. Etliche Schlösser wie Mühlbach oder Wiedendorf widmen sich neuen Ideen der Gartengestaltung; die ‚Arche Noah' bei Schloss Schiltern ist ohnedies längst zu einer Pilgerstätte für alle Naturgarten-Freunde geworden.

Auch zeitgenössische Kunst hat im Kamptal ihre Heimstätte gefunden. Das Schloss Buchberg beherbergt aktuelle konstruktivistische Kunstwerke, das Projekt ‚Land Art' bei Tautendorf präsentiert Objekte in freier Natur, rund um Langenlois finden sich zeitgenössische Kunstwerke im öffentlichen Raum. Daneben existieren freilich noch viele andere, historische Baudenkmäler. Gotische Kirchen und barocke Bildstöcke gehören selbstverständlich dazu, ebenso aber Kellerzeilen, Kellergassen, ja ganze Kellerdörfer. Sie sind integraler Teil der durch den Weinbau geprägten Kulturlandschaft, harmonisch ins Weinland eingebettete Erinnerungs-stücke an eine vergangene oder soeben vergehende Zeit.

Das LOISIUM ist, um es nochmals zu sagen, für diesen bemerkenswerten Land-strich ebenso wie für den Weinbau insgesamt zu so etwas wie einer neuen Mitte geworden. Es bereichert Stadt und Region nicht nur im übertragenen Sinn. Es unterhält und informiert, es vermittelt Genuss, Lebensfreude und macht einfach Spaß. Es konfrontiert aber vor allem, wie ein Kritiker formulierte, eine nach wie vor ländlich gebliebene Gegend mit zeitgemäßen, urbanen Standards.

Das ist, mit aller Vorsicht gesagt, die vielleicht größte Leistung, die das Objekt vollbringt, und zwar tagtäglich. Diese Spannung – spektakuläre neue Architektur

In addition, contemporary art has found a home in the Kamp Valley. Buchberg Castle houses current constructivist works of art; the 'Land Art' project in Tautendorf presents objects in the out-of-doors. All around Langelois are contem-porary works of art displayed in public spaces. But next to these are many other historical building monuments. These include without a doubt the Gothic churches and Baroque wayside shrines, but also the cellar rows, lanes and even entire cellar villages. They are an integral part of the cultural landscape which has been formed by viticulture, remembrances of a past and now fleeting era, harmoniously embedded in the wine country.

The LOISIUM—to say it once again—has become a type of new center for both this remarkable area of the country as well as for viticulture as a whole. It enriches both city and region, and not only in the figurative sense. It entertains and informs; it conveys enjoyment, joie de vivre—and is also simple fun. But above all, as one critic has claimed, it confronts an area which is still rural with modern, urban standards.

And this is, to put it carefully, perhaps the greatest achievement of the object, and one which it repeats daily. The tension between spectacular architecture and a naturally conservative small town arouses interest, stimulates discussion, and demands discourse.

This book aims to do exactly that: encourage dialogue. It aims to help one in the approach to architecture, form, and content with the appropriate precision.

in einer naturgemäß konservativen Kleinstadt – weckt Interesse, stiftet Diskussion und verlangt nach Diskurs.

Das vorliegende Buch will genau das: den Dialog befördern. Es will dabei helfen, sich der Architektur, der Form und dem Inhalt in angemessener Genauigkeit zu nähern. Dass bei jeder Nachdenk-Arbeit, bei jeder Debatte ein Glas Wein zusätzlich anregend und befruchtend wirken kann, versteht sich dabei fast von selbst, soll aber zum guten Schluss – in vino veritas! – doch nochmals gesondert betont werden. Denn schließlich steht das LOISIUM inmitten von Weingärten. Und nicht im weltfernen Niemandsland.

It is practically a given that for contemplative tasks and debate, a glass of wine may also help to inspire and fertilize. But in conclusion, it should again be singled out for emphasis: in vino veritas! Ultimately, the LOISIUM stands in the middle of vineyards, and not in the middle of nowhere.

Nächste Seiten: Weinterrassen im Kamptal; New York City, Manhattan, Madison Avenue
Following pages: Terraced vineyards in Kamp Valley; New York City, Manhattan, Madison Avenue

Gudrun Hausegger

Von Gebetsmühlen, Silberwürfeln und schwebenden Hotels

Langenlois – New York

Schauplatz *Langenlois*: Weingärten soweit das Auge reicht in akribisch paralleler Reihung. Erdige Farben, sattes Grün. Mittendrin die barocke Silhouette der niederösterreichischen Weinstadt. Am Rande der langgestreckten Stadt, inmitten ausgedehnter Weingärten, das LOISIUM: Ein ‚schwebendes' Hotel sowie ein gekippter Aluminiumkubus als Eingangsgebäude in multimedial inszenierte Weinkeller. Hotel und Eingangsgebäude entwarf der amerikanische Architekt Steven Holl, die unterirdische Kellerwelt gestaltete die Schweizer Gestaltungsagentur Steiner Sarnen Schweiz. Ein weiteres prestigeverdächtiges Projekt im Fahrwasser der aktuellen Inflation an Marketingmechanismen, die zunehmend Typologien wie Hotels und Läden mit internationaler Architektur koppeln? Dieses Urteil drängt sich vorschnell auf, besonders wenn es sich um das Thema Wein handelt. Denn seitdem Wein zunehmend zum Kulturgut avanciert, findet sein Lebenszyklus (Produktion, Vermarktung, Genuss) verstärkt in Liaison mit qualitativ hochwertiger Architektur statt. Doch geht man der eigenwilligen Anfangsdynamik dieses vielteiligen Projekts nach, entfalten sich Beweggründe, die tatsächlich unbeeinflusst von trendigen Motiven waren.

Den Anlass zum LOISIUM gab ein uralter, nicht mehr genutzter Weinkeller, in dessen Besitz Tuula und Gerhard Nidetzky 1994 mit dem Kauf eines

visionen aus dem löss
visions from the loess

Of Prayer Wheels, Silver Cubes, and Hovering Hotels

Langenlois – New York

First scene *Langenlois*: Vineyards as far as the eye can see, the vines precisely arranged in neat parallel rows, earthy colors and a rich green. And, at the center, the Baroque silhouette of the Lower Austrian wine-growing town. At the edge of this stretched-out town, amidst extensive vineyards stands the LOISIUM. A 'hovering' hotel and a tilted aluminum cube as the entrance building to the wine cellars which are the focus of a multi-media presentation. The hotel and entrance buildings were designed by American architect Steven Holl, whereas the Swiss design agency Steiner Sarnen Schweiz was responsible for the design of the underground world of the cellars. Is this just one more potentially prestigious project following in the wake of the current inflation of marketing mechanisms that increasingly couples typologies such as hotels and shops with international architecture? This hasty assessment is what immediately occurs to one, especially as we are dealing here with the theme of wine. Ever since wine began to become a cultural element its life-cycle (production, marketing, tasting) has increasingly been entering into a liaison with high-quality architecture. But on investigating the highly individual initial dynamics of this complex project we discover motives that were uninfluenced by trendy ideas. The initiative behind the LOISIUM was provided by a wine cellar no longer in use

22

1 Ein *Ackerbürgerhaus* ist eine Sonderform des Bürgerhauses, das der ‚Ackerbürger' bewohnte, der neben Acker- und Weinbau meist auch Handel trieb (darauf begründet sich auch zum Teil der Wohlstand, der an den Häusern erkennbar ist). In Niederösterreich ist dieser Typus in vielen Städten und Märkten weit verbreitet.

2 Als ‚Design-Hotels' verstehen sich weltweit über 140 unabhängig geführte Hotels, die sich durch innovatives Design auszeichnen.

Ackerbürgerhauses im historischen Zentrum von Langenlois kamen.[1] Wie an so viele der Weinbauernhöfe war dieser ganz einfach an das Haus angeschlossen. Erst das neue Eigentum regte zum Nachdenken über mögliche Nutzungen an. Vorab war nicht zwingend an einen kommerziellen Nutzen gedacht. Schritt für Schritt verfestigte sich in der Folge der Plan, die Kellergewölbe der Öffentlichkeit zugänglich zu machen und diese so zum Ausgangspunkt eines zielorientiert nutzbaren, inhaltlich kompakten Gesamtensembles zu machen. Mit dem Blick auf Langenlois als Zentrum einer traditionsreichen Weinbaugegend, waren die Zielvorgaben bald klar: Das Projekt müsse Potenzial haben, sich als wirtschaftlicher Impuls für die gesamte Region auszuwirken.

Und dieser Anspruch ist seit der Eröffnung des Besucherzentrums und der Kellerwelt 2003 sowie des Hotels 2005 durchaus gelungen: Die Weinattraktion ist mit ihrem eigenständigen Profil innerhalb der internationalen Erlebnislandschaften fix positioniert. Das Hotel, als Wine & Spa Resort geführt, wurde 2006 in den Kreis der ‚Design-Hotels' aufgenommen und mit dem ‚European Hotel Design Award' ausgezeichnet.[2] Es gilt mittlerweile als eine unumgängliche Destination für die Architekturwelt.

Die journalistische Fachwelt teilte sich angesichts des vielgestaltigen LOISIUM in kontroversielle Lager, im Schussfeuer lag das Eingangsgebäude, dem man jegliche Integrationsfähigkeit in seine einzigartige Umgebung absprach. Auch für die örtliche Bevölkerung war diese für diesen Landstrich nicht ganz alltägliche

which came into the possession of Tuula and Gerhard Nidetzky in 1995 when they acquired an *Ackerbürgerhaus* in the historic center of Langenlois.[1] As with so many of the winegrowers' houses the cellar was simply attached to the building. This new acquisition led to reflections about possible uses for the space. Initially, commercial use was not seen as essential. But step-by-step a plan crystallised to open the vaulted cellars to the public and to make this the starting point of an ensemble, compact in terms of content and usable in goal-oriented ways. With the view of Langenlois as the center of a winegrowing area with a rich tradition, the objectives soon became clear. It was seen that the project must have the potential to function as an economic impulse for the entire region.

Since the opening of the visitors' center and the *Kellerwelt* (cellar world) in 2003, followed by the hotel in 2005, this objective has been reached: this wine-based attraction with its particular character has achieved an established position in the international world of theme parks. In 2006 the hotel, which is run as a wine & spa resort, was accepted into the circle of 'Design Hotels' and was given the European Hotel Design Award.[2] A visit there is now regarded as a 'must' by those from the world of architecture.

Confronted with the polymorphic nature of the LOISIUM the journalist world split into opposing camps. The entrance building was the target for attacks that asserted it could never be integrated into the unique surroundings. For the local population, too, this kind of architecture—which is not exactly commonplace in

1 An *Ackerbürgerhaus* is a particular form of town-dweller's house inhabited by the *Ackerbürger*, who in addition to farming and winegrowing also worked in trade (which formed part of the basis for their prosperity that is reflected in their houses). In Lower Austria this type is widespread in many towns and market-towns.

2 'Design Hotels' form a loose group of over 140 independently run hotels that are characterized by their use of innovative design.

Architektur eine Herausforderung. Dass sich die anfängliche Skepsis in Akzeptanz verwandelte, hängt sicherlich nicht allein mit den Erfolgszahlen zusammen. Eine viel größere Rolle spielt – und das ist auch die Stärke des Projekts – der allumfassende Bezug zum lokalen Hab und Gut, dem Wein. Einen artfremden Inhalt gab es in den Überlegungen der Initiatoren auch nie. Nicht nur, weil der österreichische Markt an nicht-authentischen Themenparks übersättigt ist, sondern weil die Bezugnahme zum Vorhandenen allein als eine sinnvolle und folgerichtige Nutzung schien.[3]

Schauplatz *New York*: Pure urbane Intensität. Das kann eine am blanken Nervengerüst zerrende Hektik bedeuten, aber auch den unentbehrlichen Rhythmus eines Pulsschlags. Für Architekt Steven Holl, der seit 1977 in New York arbeitet, bedeutet es Letzteres. In seinem Büro im 11. Stock in Midtown Manhattan bündeln sich die Energien der Stadt.

Für Holl geht jedoch auch vom jeweiligen Ort, an dem sein Gebäude entstehen wird, der gleiche lebensnotwendige Pulsschlag aus. Er sucht ihn auf, um den eingeschriebenen – sichtbaren oder unsichtbaren – Wesenheiten nachzuspüren. Der Bauplatz in Langenlois – das LOISIUM ist übrigens Holls erster Bau in Österreich – mit seiner ureigenen Historie schien wie geschaffen für den Architekten aus New York. Holl begreift den Wein als die ortsspezifische Kraft und macht das Grundrisslabyrinth der Weinkeller zum konzeptuellen Grundmotiv der beiden Bauten. Er transformiert die jahrhundertealte unterirdische Stadt in seine ihm eigene

3 Generell wird der für eine in Österreich erfolgreiche Inszenierung notwendige regionale Bezug schon seit längerem prognostiziert (siehe Beiträge in Fachzeitschriften wie *Tourismus Magazin* 02/2004).

this region—represented a challenge. The fact that the initial scepticism gradually transformed into acceptance is certainly not due to the success figures alone. It is the all-embracing relationship to the local source of wealth, wine, that has played a far greater role. Nor did the initiators ever consider contents that would be foreign to the area, this was not only because the Austrian market is saturated with unauthentic theme parks, but because relating to what already existed seemed the only sensible and logical use.[3]

Next scene *New York*: Pure urban intensity. This can mean a hectic pace that tears at frayed nerves, but can also mean the indispensable rhythm of the pulse. For architect Steven Holl, who has worked in New York since 1977, it is the latter. In his office on the eleventh floor in midtown Manhattan the energies of the city are concentrated.

But for Holl the same pulse beat that is essential for life comes from the place where his building will be erected. He searches for it to discover the inscribed— visible or invisible—essence. The site in Langenlois (the LOISIUM is Holl's first building in Austria) with its very particular history seemed to have been made for this New York architect. Holl sees wine as the force that is specific to the place and makes the labyrinthine floor plan of the wine cellar into the basic conceptual motif for both buildings. He translates the centuries-old underground town into his own formal idiom, thus creating a referential contrast between contemporary architecture and the ancient existing substance that is typical of his work. This

3 Generally speaking the kind of regional reference necessary for a successful presentation in Austria has been forecast for a considerable time (see contributions in specialist journals such as *Tourismus Magazin* 02/2004).

Visionen aus dem Löss

Visions from the Loess

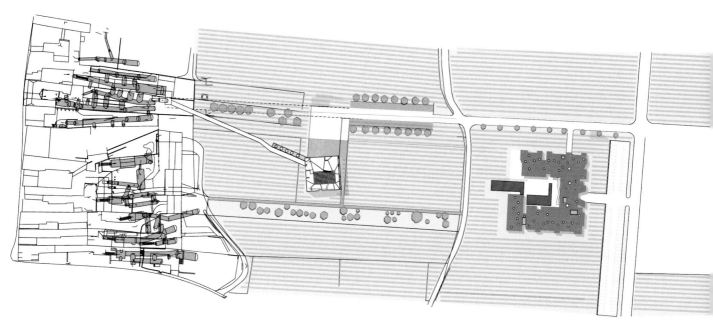

Situationsplan mit Kellerröhren,
Besucherzentrum und Hotel
Site plan showing cellar vaults,
visitors' center and hotel

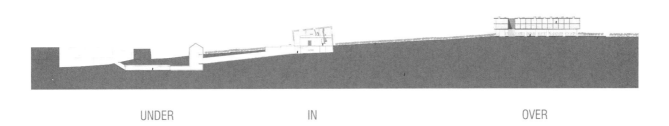

UNDER   IN   OVER

Schnitt durch das Gesamtareal
Site section

Formensprache und erzeugt so den für ihn typischen referenziellen Gegensatz von zeitgenössischer Architektur und Uraltem, Bestehenden. Ein Gegensatz, der sich in die zahlreichen Gegensätzlichkeiten des Landstrichs nahtlos fügt: Die landschaftlichen Gegebenheiten mit ihren vielfältigen Vegetations- und Boden-formationen; die unterschiedlichen klimatischen Verhältnisse und die uralte Kulturlandschaft eines Weinanbaugebiets mit starken Kontrasten, wie die hoch technisierten Weinbaubetriebe auf der einen Seite, die alten Kellergassen mit ihren Winzerhäusern und in den Löss geduckten Weinkellern auf der anderen Seite. So stimmig sich diese Landschaft der Gegensätze präsentiert, so stimmig nimmt man auch die Atmosphäre der so unterschiedlichen Bauten von Besucherzentrum und Hotel wahr. Warum? ‚Es ist ein Wurf aus einer Hand. Man kann von einem Gesamtkunstwerk sprechen', meint der Bauherr.[4] Denn Steven Holl zeichnet für den Masterplan, die architektonische Gestaltung bis hin zum Design von Möbeln und Türgriffen verantwortlich. Nur so konnte der gewisse urbane Zug, der so typisch für manches der tonangebenden New Yorker Hotels ist, bis in die Hotel-lobby in Langenlois seine Fortsetzung finden.

Warum Ideen wahr werden
‚Dass wir an eine Nutzbarmachung der Weinkeller dachten, lag auf der Hand. Denn diese Keller sind Kunstwerke und gehen verloren, wenn sie nicht gepflegt werden. Durch die Kraft der Wurzeln von Weinstöcken und Bäumen ist die Gefahr

[4] Laut Gespräch mit Tuula und Gerhard Nidetzky, Oktober 2006

contrast fits seamlessly among the numerous existing contrasts in this area. The characteristics of the landscape with its varied forms of vegetation and ground, the different climatic conditions, and the ancient cultivated landscape of a wine-growing area with strong contrasts, such as the highly technological business of winegrowing on the one hand, and the old *Kellergassen* (literally: cellar lanes) with the winegrowers' houses and the wine-cellars tucked into the loess on the other. Just as this landscape of contrasts presents a harmonious appearance, the atmos-phere exuded by the visitors' center and the hotel, which are very different buildings, is also experienced as harmonious. Why is this? 'Because it is a design made by a single hand. One could speak here of a *gesamtkunstwerk*,' says the client.[4] Steven Holl was responsible for the master plan, the architectural design and also the design of the furniture down to the door handles. This explains how that certain urban trait, so typical of some of New York's leading hotels, could extend as far as the hotel lobby in Langenlois.

Why Ideas become Real
'It was obvious that we thought of finding a use for the wine cellars. They are a kind of artwork and if they are not looked after they can be lost. The strength of the roots of the vines and trees means that the danger of collapse is consider-able. Today nobody can re-erect a Gothic or Baroque wine-cellar. And these eras are represented in the system of cellars under Langenlois,' Gerhard Nidetzky

[4] According to a conversation with Tuula and Gerhard Nidetzky, October 2006

des Einsturzes groß. Aber kein Mensch kann heute einen gotischen oder barocken Keller wieder aufbauen. Und all diese Epochen sind in diesen Kellersystemen unter Langenlois vertreten. Unter unserem Haus liegen zum Beispiel 900 Jahre alte Gewölbe', erzählt Gerhard Nidetzky mit einer Selbstverständlichkeit, als ob es sich bei dem Vorhaben, 900 Jahre alte Keller nutzbar zu machen, um einen kleinen Garagenumbau handelt.[5]

Man muss schon das persönliche Profil dieses Bauherrn genauer kennen, um so ein Ansinnen samt konsequenter Umsetzung einordnen zu können. Da ist zunächst einmal die enge persönliche Verbundenheit mit dem Ort: Gerhard Nidetzky, im nahen Schönberg am Kamp als Sohn einer Winzerfamilie geboren, hat mit seiner Entscheidung, in Wien zu studieren, dem Wein zunächst den Rücken zugekehrt. Dann die rasche und erfolgreiche Karriere als Steuerberater und Wirtschaftstreuhänder mit großem Interesse für Kunst und Kultur. So wird er oftmals skizziert. Doch irgendwie ist dieses Bild unscharf, vielleicht gerade deshalb, weil es so auf die Profession fokussiert ist. Vielmehr sollte man von einem Humanisten gediegener, alter Schule sprechen, der professionelle und persönliche Fähigkeiten und Neigungen in steter Synergie wirken lässt. Die ähnlich gelagerte Dynamik seiner Frau Tuula, einer gebürtigen Finnin, verstärkt diese Synergien in perfekter Ergänzung. Mit exakt diesem ganzheitlichen Zugang, ihrem großen persönlichen Einsatz und Interesse, begleiteten beide das Projekt LOISIUM. Selbstverständlich die visionäre Triebfeder immer im Gepäck mit dabei. Allein vor diesem Hintergrund

5 Ibid.

recounts in a perfectly natural way, as if the project of making 900-year old cellars usable once again were nothing more than a small garage conversion.[5]

To properly classify a project like this and the consistent way in which it has been implemented, one has to establish a better knowledge of the character and biography of this client. First of all there is the close personal connection to the place. Gerhard Nidetzky, who was born nearby in Schönberg am Kamp as the son of a winegrowing family, initially turned his back on wine when he decided to study in Vienna. This was followed by a rapid and successful career as a tax consultant and accountant with a deep interest in art and culture. Or rather, this is the career outline that is often cited, but somehow or other this picture is blurred, perhaps because it focuses so much on the profession. Perhaps one should talk more of a humanist of the grand old school who allows professional and personal abilities and inclinations to function in constant synergy. His wife Tuula, born in Finland, has a similar dynamic and thus strengthens these synergies as a perfect complement. With this holistic approach, immense personal commitment and interest, this couple pursued the LOISIUM project—naturally always with the visionary mainspring in their intellectual luggage. It is only against this background that it seemed 'obvious,' as Nidetzky puts it, to persuade the neighbors, who also had a similar network of cellars, to combine their underground property and then philosophize together about new ideas for the cellars. Convincing the winegrowing families Haimerl on the one side and

5 Ibid.

ist es verständlich, dass ‚es naheliegend war', so Nidetzky, auch die Nachbarn, die über ein gleiches Netz an Kellern verfügten, für eine Zusammenlegung des unterirdischen Guts zu gewinnen, um dann gemeinsam über neue Kellerideen zu philosophieren. Die Winzerfamilien Haimerl auf der einen Seite und Steininger auf der anderen Seite waren beide nicht schwer zu überzeugen. Offensichtlich wohnt da Tür an Tür der gleiche visionäre Mut, der sich auch durch den vorherzusehenden persönlichen finanziellen Einsatz nicht abschrecken ließ. Vorausgeschickt werden muss, dass die Familie Steininger ihren Produktionsbetrieb in die Kellerwelt integrieren wird.

Für die drei Nachbarn folgten zunächst ausgedehnte regionale und internationale Feldforschungen (wie Retzer Kellerwelt, Londoner Weinerlebniswelt Vinopolis, Weinkeller in Bordeaux und der Champagne), um Vorbilder für eine mögliche Nutzung dieses unterirdischen Stadtraumes mit immerhin einen Kilometer Länge zu finden. Parallel dazu wurden auch Entwürfe einheimischer Szenografen eingeholt. Anregungen gab es nach dieser intensiven Ideensuche viele, konkrete Vorbilder oder eine zündende Idee allerdings noch nicht. Der Anspruch, eine qualitativ hochwertige und thematisch authentische Bespielung zu visualisieren, blieb einstweilen noch ohne inhaltliche Antwort.

Doch dann begann einer dieser ‚wundersamen Zufälle' zu wirken, die dem Projekt in der Folge noch öfter zugute kamen und die Inszenierung in der Kufsteiner Glasfabrik Riedel – des renommierten österreichischen Weinglasherstellers –

Steininger on the other was not difficult. Clearly these neighbors shared much the same kind of visionary courage and did not allow themselves to be deterred by the foreseeable personal financial commitment. It should be said first that the Steininger family will integrate their production business in the cellar world.

For these three neighbors what followed next was extensive regional and international field research (such as the *Retz Kellerwelt*, the London wine experience world, *Vinopolis*, wine cellars in Bordeaux and Champagne), to discover models for a possible use of this underground urban space with a length of a kilometer. Parallel to this designs were obtained from native scenographers. Following this intensive search for ideas there were many suggestions and stimuli but, as yet, no concrete models or convincing ideas.

But then one of these 'wondrous coincidences' that subsequently were often to guide the development of this project occurred and attention was drawn to the presentation in the Kufstein glass factory of Riedel—the world-renowned Austrian wineglass manufacturer.[6] It was discovered that a Swiss agency with the resonant name of Steiner Sarnen Schweiz had been responsible. So the Nidetzkys went on tour again and immersed themselves in the experience world of this Swiss Team: in the *Sinnfonie* of the glassworks in Kufstein, in a glass museum as well as in an urban refuse incineration plant, the latter in Hergiswil in Switzerland on the shores of Lake Lucerne. In all these projects the focus was on explaining history by

6 At the visitors' center pre-opening event in September 2003 Dietmar Steiner talked of 'wondrous coincidences' that often occurred in the LOISIUM project.

ins Blickfeld rückte.[6] Eine Schweizer Agentur mit dem klingenden Namen Steiner Sarnen Schweiz sei da am Werk gewesen. So gingen die Nidetzkys erneut auf Tournee und tauchten ein in die Erlebniswelten des Schweizer Teams: in die ‚Sinnfonie' der Glashütte in Kufstein, in ein Glasmuseum sowie in eine städtische Müllverbrennungsanlage, die beiden letzteren im schweizerischen Hergiswil am Ufer des Vierwaldstätter Sees gelegen. Überall standen die Vermittlung von Geschichten durch verdichtete, räumliche Inszenierungen, multimediale, phanta-stische Reisen, ausgeräumte Barrieren zwischen den ausgestellten Objekten und den Betrachtern und stattdessen ein aktives Publikum im Vordergrund. Information durch Erlebnis und Kurzweil, das sind die Grundpfeiler der Gestaltungsethik von Otto J. Steiner, dem Begründer von Steiner Sarnen Schweiz. Die Art, wie die Schweizer Gestalter die Essenz eines Ortes einfangen und daraus Botschaften entwickeln, gefiel. Und Steiner selbst überzeugte durch die Allgegenwart seiner Visionen, die es gilt, in tagtäglicher Herausforderung auf den Boden zu bringen. Einer Zusammenarbeit stand nichts im Wege und bereits im April 1999 präsentierte Otto J. Steiner in Langenlois eine erste Konzeptidee für eine Bespielung der Keller.

Vor dem Bau

Um die Rahmenbedingungen dieses ehrgeizigen Vorhabens durchzuführen, waren in der Folge zahlreiche organisatorische Schritte abzuwickeln. Vor allem sollte die Kellerwelt ein adäquates, repräsentatives Eingangsgebäude erhalten.

6 Dietmar Steiner sprach beim Pre-Opening zur Eröffnung des Besucherzentrums im September 2003 von ‚wundersamen Zufällen', die beim Projekt LOISIUM oftmals mitwirkten.

means of compressed, spatial presentations, fantastical multimedia voyages, removing barriers between the objects and the viewers and actively involving the public. Otto J. Steiner, the founder of Steiner Sarnen Schweiz, bases his design ethic on communicating information through experience and amusement. The way in which the Swiss designers capture the essence of a place and develop messages out of it proved appealing. And Steiner himself was convincing through the omnipresence of his visions, which need to be brought down to earth by day-to-day challenges. There were no obstacles to collaboration and in April 1999 Otto J. Steiner presented his first conceptual idea for the use of the cellars in Langenlois.

Before the Building

Numerous organisational steps had to be taken to establish the framework for this ambitious project. Above all a suitable and impressive entrance building needed to be provided for the cellar world. Steiner Sarnen Schweiz, who were responsible for the organisation of the architecture competition, received expert advice from Dietmar Steiner, the director of the Architekturzentrum Wien. Subsequently involved in the project as architecture consultant, Steiner initially examined the preferences and tastes of the clients. They wanted a calm architec-ture, their preferred material was wood, and they wanted nothing spectacular, but something clear and reserved in the Scandinavian tradition. The competition

Steiner Sarnen Schweiz, verantwortlich für die Organisation eines Architekten-Wettbewerbs, holten fachkundigen Rat bei Dietmar Steiner, dem Direktor des Architekturzentrum Wien. In weiterer Folge als Architektur-Konsulent in das Projekt eingebunden, diagnostizierte dieser zunächst Vorlieben und Geschmäcker der BauherrInnen: Eine ruhige Architektur war gewünscht. Die bevorzugte Materialsprache Holz. Nichts Spektakuläres, eher etwas Klares, Zurückhaltendes im Sinne skandinavischer Tradition. Zur Ausschreibung des Wettbewerbs kam es nicht, da die Rede zuvor auf Steven Holls Kiasma Museum of Contemporary Art in Helsinki fiel, das Tuula Nidetzky kannte und auch sehr schätzte. So etwas in Langenlois zu haben, das wäre schon eine Sache. So konfrontierte Dietmar Steiner bei einem folgenden New York-Besuch (das Architekturzentrum Wien bereitete zu dieser Zeit eine Ausstellung über Steven Holl vor) den Architekten mit der Aufgabenstellung. Holl, über die Auftraggeber informiert, stimmte zu.

Im März 2001 ist es dann soweit: Steven Holl kommt zum ersten Lokalaugenschein nach Langenlois, besichtigt und studiert Bauplatz und Umgebung. Er skizziert erste Vorschläge für einen Masterplan, der sich als erstaunlich ausgereift erweisen wird und auch die bestimmende Verortung der drei Bauteile bereits enthält: *under the ground* (die Kellerwelt) – *in the ground* (das Eingangsgebäude) und *above the ground* (das Hotel). Die Magie der ersten Skizze zieht die Auftraggeber in ihren Bann, gleichfalls ist aber auch der New Yorker Architekt fasziniert von der Magie des Ortes und schließlich auch von der hohen Weinkultur, der Differenziertheit

was never organized, as beforehand Steven Holl's Kiasma Museum of Contemporary Art in Helsinki cropped up in conversation, a building that Tuula Nidetzky knew and also greatly liked. To have something like this in Langenlois would be a fine thing, it was thought. And so during a visit to New York (around this time the Architekturzentrum Wien was planning an exhibition about Steven Holl) Dietmar Steiner confronted the architect with this commission. Holl, having been informed about the clients, agreed.

In March 2001 the time had come: Steven Holl comes for his first site inspection to Langenlois, studies the site and the surroundings. He sketches his first proposals for a master plan that turns out to be extraordinarily developed and already determines the placing of the three parts of the building: *under the ground* (the cellar world), *in the ground* (the entrance building) and *above the ground* (the hotel). The magic of the first sketches fascinates the client, while at the same time the New York architect is fascinated by the magic of the place and ultimately also by the sophisticated wine culture, the many different types, vintages, and ways of making wine.

In July Steven Holl and Steiner Sarnen Schweiz present the preliminary design to the council, the officials responsible and the very enthusiastic mayor.

Permission is granted. As the final step Viennese architects Irene Ott-Reinisch and Franz Sam (the latter worked for many years for Coop Himmelb(l)au and was thus eminently qualified in the implementation of complex building commissions) joined the team as the local site architects.

an Sorten, Jahrgängen und Ausbau. Im Juli präsentieren Steven Holl und
Steiner Sarnen Schweiz den Vorentwurf bereits vor der Gemeinde, zuständigen
Verantwortlichen und einem sehr wohlwollenden Bürgermeister. Das Go wird
ausgesprochen. Als letzter Schritt werden die Wiener ArchitektInnen Irene
Ott-Reinisch und Franz Sam (als ehemaliger Mitarbeiter von Coop Himmelb(l)au
bestens qualifiziert für Umsetzungen komplexer Bauaufgabe) als lokale aus-
führende Architekten in das Team aufgenommen.

Meilensteine der Baustelle

Das Szenario: Drei Baustellen (zwei davon zeitgleich, aber voneinander unabhängig
geführt), knappe Planungs- und Bauzeiten, sowie bautechnische Herausforderungen unterschiedlichster Art und Weise.[7]
Baustelle *under the ground*, die Kellerwelt: Beim Bau der Weinerlebniswelt unter
der Leitung von Diplomingenieur Andreas Gattermann wurden teils die bestehenden Kellerröhren adaptiert, teils wurden Abschnitte bzw. Verbindungsgänge
neu errichtet. Der prinzipielle Anspruch beim Umbau lautete, einerseits den
Bestand mit altem Material (Ziegel, Putz) zu rekonstruieren, andererseits das
Neue als neu darzustellen. Ein technischer Meilenstein der unterirdischen Bau-
stelle war sicherlich der Einbau des neuen Produktionsbetriebs der Familie
Steininger, der als zweigeschossige Anlage zwischen die umseitig anschließenden
Kellerröhren regelrecht eingepasst wurde. Um ein neues Zwischengeschoss

7 Für alle Informationen in diesem
Kapitel gilt mein ausdrücklicher
Dank Irene Ott-Reinisch, Franz
Sam, Bernd Leopold und Andreas
Gattermann, Gespräche
Oktober – Dezember 2006.

Milestones of the Building Site
The scenario: three building sites (two of them run at the same time but independently of each other), tight planning and construction schedules, as well as
building construction challenges of the most varied kind.[7]
Building site *under the ground*, the cellar world: in constructing this wine experience world under the supervision of Diplomingenieur Andreas Gatterman,
the existing cellar passageways were adapted in part, while new sections and
connections were also made. The principal aim in the conversion was on the one
hand to reconstruct the existing substance using old materials (brick, plaster)
while on the other hand to present the new substance as such.
One technical milestone in the underground building site was certainly the incor-
poration of the production business of the Steininger family that was 'fitted-in'
in the form of a two-story complex between the cellar passageways adjoining on
all sides. To be able to make a new mezzanine level (for cold storage and filling
facilities) above the basement (where the steel tanks stand) the ground had to
be removed which meant that the normally even load over the cellar vaults was
subject to constant change and the stability was threatened. Temporary supports
and complex spanning techniques prevented the collapse of the vaults. Only
in this way was it possible to remove the four to five meters of earth without the
building machinery—that had to operate close above the old vaults—causing
the collapse of the tunnels.

7 For all the information in this
chapter my special thanks are due
to Irene Ott-Reinisch, Franz Sam,
Bernd Leopold and Andreas
Gattermann, these conversations
took place between October and
December 2006.

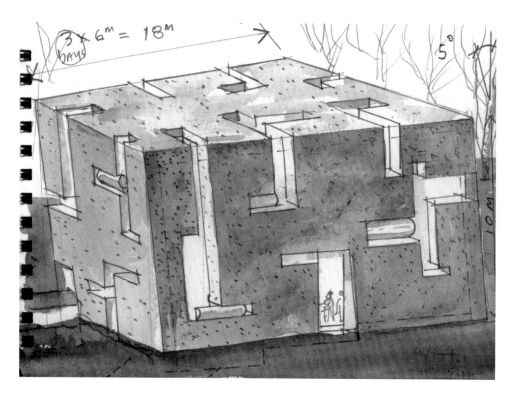

Steven Holl, Entwurfszeichnung
Besucherzentrum
Steven Holl, design drawing
visitors' center

Besucherzentrum, Grundrisse
1. Obergeschoss und Erdgeschoss
Visitors' center, floor plan of the
first floor and of the basement

Steven Holl, Entwurfszeichnung
Besucherzentrum
Steven Holl, design drawing
visitors' center

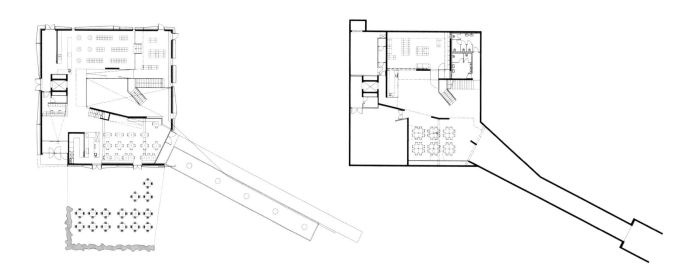

(für Kühllager und Abfüllanlage) über dem Kellergeschoss (dort lagern heute die Stahltanks) einführen zu können, musste Erdreich abgetragen werden, wodurch aber die sonst gleichmäßige Belastung über den Kellergewölben ständigen Änderungen ausgesetzt war und die Stabilität gefährdet wurde. Temporäre Abstützungen und komplizierte Verspannungen verhinderten ein Einbrechen der Gewölbe. Nur so war es möglich, dass vier bis fünf Meter Erdreich darüber abgetragen werden konnte und die Baumaschinen, die knapp über den alten Gewölben agierten, diese nicht zum Einsturz brachten.

Baustelle *Besucherzentrum*: Die technische Komplexität sowie die kurze Bauzeit von zwölf Monaten von Besucherzentrum und Hotel setzten ein perfekt koordiniertes und rasches Zusammenspiel voraus zwischen dem Büro Steven Holl in New York unter dem Projektleiter Christian Wassmann und den ausführenden ArchitektInnen Franz Sam und Irene Ott-Reinisch samt ihrem Team in Wien bzw. in Langenlois. Neben einer 24-Stunden-Schicht (aufgeteilt auf die zeitversetzten Arbeitsphasen in Wien und New York) war permanent das konstruktiv-technische, aber auch logistische Know-How von Ott-Reinisch und Sam gefordert.

Beim Bau des Besucherzentrums war das Wiener Team mit einem groß dimensionierten und leicht gekippten ‚Einraum' mit 7.330 m³ Kubatur konfrontiert, dessen dünne, 17 m hohe Stahlbetonwände zusätzlich noch irregulär penetriert waren. Warum? Steven Holl übertrug das System der unterirdischen Kellerröhren – das ideelle Fundament seines Entwurfs – in Form von tiefen Einschnitten direkt auf

Building site *visitors' center*: the technical complexity as well as the short construction period of twelve months for the visitors' center and the hotel demanded perfectly coordinated and speedy collaboration between the office of Steven Holl in New York under project leader Christian Wassmann and the site architects Franz Sam and Irene Ott-Reinisch with their team in Vienna and Langenlois. In addition to a 24 hour shift (divided to cover the time difference between working hours in Vienna and New York) the constructional, technical and also logistical know-how of Ott-Reinisch and Sam was constantly tested.

In building the visitors' center the Vienna team was confronted with a large, slightly tilted 'single space' with a cubage of 7,330 m³, with thin, 17-meter tall reinforced concrete walls that, in addition, were penetrated by openings at irregular intervals. Why? Steven Holl transferred the system of the underground cellar tunnels—the conceptual foundation of his design—in the form of direct incisions in the façade of the building.

To execute this sculptural building, which, additionally, was inserted up to a third of its height in the depths of the loess—*in the ground*—suggested that the construction process would be a turbulent one. It was not only that the thin concrete walls with, in places, deep incisions, the large spans, the heavy reinforcement and the extreme concrete pour heights meant a structural challenge. Additionally working in stages combined with the inclined walls constantly altered the overall stability of the building, making the use of external supports necessary. Above

die Fassade des Baukörpers. Diesen skulpturalen Baukörper zu realisieren, der noch dazu zu einem Drittel in den Tiefen des Löss – *in the ground* – steckte, versprach einen turbulenten Bauprozess: Nicht nur, dass die dünnen, teilweise tief eingeschnittenen Betonwände, die großen Spannweiten sowie eine starke Bewehrung und extreme Betonfüllhöhen eine statische Herausforderung bedeuteten. Zudem verschob sich durch das abschnittsweise Arbeiten und die schrägen Wände ständig die Gesamtstabilität. Abstützungen von außen waren notwendig. Vor allem die um fünf Grad geneigte Südwand erreichte erst mit dem Einzug der Decke ihre Endstabilität. Ein innovatives technisches Bravourstück gelang mit der Verglasung der Aussparungen, die teilweise über die Dachkante gezogen wurden. Deshalb wurden die Fensterstöcke zunächst im Rohbau mitbetoniert. Dann kamen, um die zahlreichen Schichten in der Vertikale mit den andersgearteten Schichten der Dachzone zu verbinden, konstruktionstechnische Transformationsglieder zum Einsatz, die das Zusammenführen ermöglichten.

Die drei Hauptmaterialien, die das Besucherzentrum bestimmen, leitete Steven Holl von den Bestandteilen einer Weinflasche ab: Grünes Glas, Kork und – bei Weinflaschen der gehobenen Klasse – eine Aluminiumabdeckung darüber. Genauso eine silberne Haut sollte auch der Würfel bekommen, die man schließlich in speziellen Marine-Aluminiumplatten (eine widerstandsfeste Legierung aus dem Schiffsbau) fand. Die exakten Planvorgaben aus dem Büro Holl verlangten ein akribisches Handanlegen an jede der 680 Platten in der Langenloiser

all the south wall that is at an angle of five degrees only achieved its final stability once the ceiling slab had been poured.

Glazing the openings, some of which are continued over the edge of the roof, involved an innovative feat of technical daring. To achieve this, the window frames were fixed before pouring the concrete structure. Then, in order to connect the numerous vertical layers of materials with the layers of quite different materials in the roof zone, elements had to be developed to make the technical transition that could bring these zones together.

The three main materials that determine the character of the visitors' center were derived by Steven Holl from the elements of a wine bottle: green glass, cork and—in wines of a better class—the aluminum cap on the cork. The cube was to be given exactly this kind of silvery skin, which was finally discovered in the form of special marine aluminum panels (a durable alloy used in shipbuilding). The exact plans from Holl's office demanded from the Langenlois metalwork firm precise handwork on each of the 680 panels used. In the factory the panels were mounted one by one onto a substructure and then numbered and delivered to the building site.

Hotel building site: in planning and erecting the hotel the challenge lay in the dramatic change of scale (four full storys and a cubage of 29,000 m³), as well as in the conceptually difficult requirement that the hotel should seem to hover—above the ground. Like in the visitors' center these requirements exerted considerable

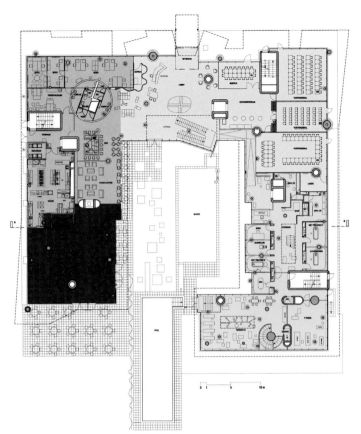

Grundriss Erdgeschoss

Floor plan of the first upper floor

Grundriss Kellergeschoss

Floor plan of the ground floor

Metallbaufirma. Eins zu eins wurden die Platten im Werk auf die Unterkonstruktion aufmontiert, nummeriert und danach auf die Baustelle geliefert.

Baustelle *Hotel*: Bei Planung und Bau des Hotels lagen die Herausforderungen neben dem Sprung in der Größenordnung (vier Vollgeschosse und eine Kubatur von 29.000 m³), auch in der konzeptuell schwierigen Aufgabe, dass das Hotel über der Erde – *above the ground* – schweben sollte. Beides forderte, wie beim Besucherzentrum, wiederum eine hohe konstruktiv-technische und logistische Leistung. Ideengeschichtliche Entwurfsvorgaben waren beim Hotel nicht nur die Formensprache, die aus den Tiefen der Kellerwelt abgezogen und auf Grundriss, Schnitt und Fassade übertragen wurde, sondern auch die Assoziation, dass ein ‚Wald von unterschiedlich starken Baumstämmen' (so Steven Holl) die beiden Obergeschosse der Gästezimmer trägt. Diese wiederum umschließt ein perforierter Aluminiummantel. Statisch gelöst wurde der Effekt des Tragens (Franz Sam spricht angesichts von ca. 2.100 m² zu tragender Grundfläche wohl richtiger von einem ‚In-die-Höhe-Stemmen') mit einer 50 cm starken Platte als Tragwerk. Deren Hauptlast wird durch 50 stark bewehrte Betonsäulen punktgestützt, die Baumstämmen gleich, vom Erdgeschoss des Rohbaus ‚emporwachsen' und auch für die Leitungsführung verwendet werden. Die Platte wird durch die drei Stiegen und Aufzugskerne zusätzlich stabilisiert. Manche der Punktstützungen sind bis zur Grenztragfähigkeit ausgelastet. Darüber hinaus muss die Platte gewährleisten, Auskragungen von bis zu sechs Meter Länge zu tragen.

demands both in terms of construction technology as well as logistics.

Design goals in the case of the hotel included not only the use of a formal idiom that was derived from the depths of the cellar world and was applied to floor plan, section and façade, but also the association that a 'forest of trees with trunks of different thicknesses' (to quote Steven Holl) carries the two upper floors with the guest bedrooms. These are in turn encased in a perforated shell of aluminum. In structural terms the effect of carrying (given the floor area of about 2,100 m² Franz Sam speaks here more correctly of 'lifting up') was solved with a 50 cm thick slab as the structure. The main load is carried by fifty heavily reinforced concrete columns that resemble tree trunks, and 'grow upwards' from the ground floor of the building and are also used to contain service runs. This slab is additionally stabilized by three staircase and lift cores. Some of the point supports are loaded to the limits of their capacity. In addition the slab must deal with cantilevers up to six meters in length.

Here too innumerable technically demanding detail solutions were demanded. For example part of the complex light concept is a way of handling light extending through several floors. From the mezzanine level a spot sends concentrated light into the spa area through a so-called *Frog-Lamp*, inserted in the floor slab of the story above. An ingenious design that, however, made it necessary to fix the position of the holes and insert the *Frog-Lamps* in the formwork before pouring the concrete for the primary structure.

Auch hier unzählige technisch fordernde Detaillösungen. Teil des komplexen Lichtkonzepts ist zum Beispiel eine mehrgeschossige Lichtführung: Vom Zwischengeschoss schickt ein Spot durch die sogenannte *Frog-Lamp*, im Boden des Geschosses darunter liegend, gebündeltes Licht in den Spa-Bereich. Ein genialer Entwurf, der allerdings schon beim Rohbau die Setzung der Löcher bzw. das Einbetonieren der *Frog-Lamp* notwendig machte.

Die eigentliche Herausforderung beim Hotelbau war trotz allem der perforierte Aluminiummantel. Der wahre Meilenstein, sozusagen: Zum einen ging die zentrale Entwurfsidee der Ummantelung von einer textilen Anmutung aus, die keine scharfkantigen Löcher zuließ, sondern abgerundete Aussparungen verlangte. Das bedeutete aber, dass nicht mit normierter Stanzung gearbeitet werden konnte, sondern eine computergesteuerte Fräse zum Einsatz kam, die auch den Vorteil hatte, dass alle Platten mit ihren in einem langwierigen Prozess festgelegten Ausschnitten (markante Punkte in der Umgebung rahmend bzw. unerwartete Ausblicke freigebend) individuell bearbeitet werden konnten. Zeitgleich zu diesen inhaltlichen Vorgaben mussten die funktionalen Anforderungen sowie eine funktional optimierte Montage bei der Umsetzung Berücksichtigung finden.

From High Above to Deep Below

Als letzter Teil des Gesamtprojekts LOISIUM fand die nahezu acht Meter hohe Skulptur *Ohne Titel* von Heimo Zobernig Platz hoch oben am Käferberg inmitten

But in the hotel building the real challenge was, despite everything, the aluminum shell. This was the true milestone so to speak. First of all the central design idea of encasing or sheathing was based on the notion of a textile that did not permit any sharp-edged holes but required rounded openings. This meant that the standard methods of press-cutting could not be used; instead a computer-operated milling cutter was used. This had the advantage that all the panels with cut-outs that had been defined through a lengthy process (they frame striking points in the surroundings or reveal unexpected views) could be worked on individually. While dealing with these constraints derived from the concept of the building, the functional requirements as well as the optimal way of fixing the panels had to be considered.

From High Above to Deep Below

As the last part of the overall LOISIUM project the sculpture *Ohne Titel* (Untitled) by Heimo Zobernig that measures almost eight meters high was given a place on the Käferberg amidst famous vineyards.[8] It was unavoidable that the local population soon associated the 130 stacked balls of untreated metal with a bunch of grapes—although probably designed by the artist as an abstract molecular structure. It is from here, with the view across the terraces to the LOISIUM below, that one can perhaps most clearly grasp the geometry of the vineyards that, according to Steven Holl, connect the hotel and the visitors' center like 'the grid of a city.'

8 The sculpture *Ohne Titel* was the first work completed in the framework of the art program *Festival der Gärten – Kamptal 2006*.

Besucherzentrum mit Hotel im
Hintergrund
Visitors' center, showing the
hotel in the background

Besucherzentrum
Visitors' center

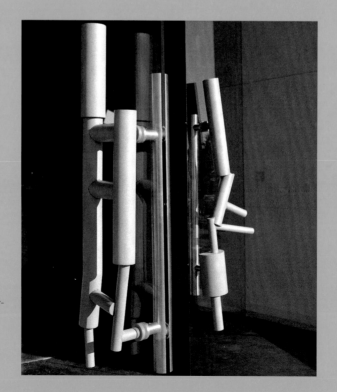

Haupteingang: Aluminium Türgriffe in Form der Kellerröhren
Main entrance: aluminum
door handle in the form of
cellar vaults

Blick auf die Fensteraus-
sparungen der Südfassade
View of the window recesses
on the south elevation

berühmter Weinrieden.[8] Unvermeidlich, dass die Bevölkerung die 130 aus unbehandeltem Stahlblech aufgetürmten Kugeln – wiewohl vom Künstler als abstrakte Molekularstruktur entworfen – bald mit einer Weintraube assoziierten. Von hier mit dem Blick hinab über die Terrassen zum LOISIUM versteht man auch am besten die Geometrie der Weingärten, die ‚wie der Raster einer Stadt', so Steven Holl, Hotel und Besucherzentrum verbinden.

Unten angelangt, in einem der Weingärten, gibt die transparente Lobby des *Hotels* den Blick über Pool und Weingarten frei bis hin zum Besucherzentrum und weiter ins Zentrum von Langenlois. Der Boden des Weingartens selbst scheint in die Lobby mit ihren gedämpften erdigen Tönen hineinzufließen. Reduzierter Luxus oder Wohligkeit durch Einfachheit, so könnte man die Stimmung bezeichnen. Atmosphäre durch klare Linien, ein gefärbter Industrieestrich und ein nuanciertes Farb- und Lichtkonzept. Die farblich differenzierten Bereiche, wie Seminarräume, Spa, Restaurant und Bar, nehmen diese Stimmung auf.

Ganz anders abgestimmt geben sich die Gästezimmer mit ihren geweißten Betonoberflächen und die Gänge mit den Spuren der rauen Bretterschalung weitaus kühler und zurückhaltender. Aber auch hier die allgegenwärtige Referenz zur Kellerwelt: Die Gänge, natürlich belichtet und hell, verlaufen leicht verwinkelt; von der Gangbeleuchtung bis hin zu den Mustern der Stoffbezüge auf den Möbeln finden sich allesamt Abbreviaturen der Kellerröhren. Mit Originalgrafiken renommierter niederösterreichischer Künstler als Zimmerausstattung werden

8 Die Skulptur *Ohne Titel* war die erste fertiggestellte Arbeit im Rahmen des Kunstprogramms *Festival der Gärten – Kamptal 2006.*

When one arrives below, in one of the vineyards, the transparent lobby of the *hotel* reveals a view of the pool and vineyards extending as far as the visitors' center and beyond that to the center of Langenlois. The ground of the vineyards appears to extend into the lobby with its muted earthy colors. The atmosphere could be described as one of reduced luxury or well-being through simplicity. Atmosphere is produced through clear lines, a colored industrial screed, and a nuanced concept of light and colors. The areas that are differentiated by the use of color, such as the seminar rooms, the spa area as well as the restaurant and the bar—take up this atmosphere.

The guest bedrooms with their whitened concrete surfaces and the corridors with the traces of the rough timber shuttering are far cooler and restrained. But here too there is the omnipresent reference to the cellar world: the corridors, which are naturally lit and bright, run at a slight angle, abbreviated versions of the cellar passageways are found throughout—from the corridor lighting to the patterns of the upholstery material. Through the use of original graphic works by well-known Lower Austrian artists as part of the furnishings regional references of another kind are developed.

The complex package of furniture and lighting is composed of individual pieces that form a harmonious overall composition and was designed by Holl's office. A few of the individual pieces such as the multi-functional elements by Frederick Kiesler in the lounge (a new edition by the Wittmann firm based in the

regionale Bezüge anderer Art aufgenommen.

Das komplexe Möbel- und Beleuchtungspaket, das sich aus Einzelstücken zu einer stimmigen Gesamtkomposition fügt, entwarf das Büro Holl. Einige Einzelfertigungen, wie die multifunktionalen Teile von Friedrich Kiesler in der Lounge (eine Neuauflage der Firma Wittmann aus dem benachbarten Etsdorf) oder die *Peanuts-Liege* im Spa-Bereich, wurden dazugenommen. ‚Die feinen, aufwendigen Materialkombinationen der Möbel aus dunklen Hölzern, schwarzem Leder und dicken Teppichen stehen in einem Dialog zu den rauen Oberflächen des Baus und garantieren Komfortgefühl', so Christian Wassmann, der für den Entwurf der Möbel verantwortlich zeichnet.[9] Betten, Polstermöbel und Stühle sind in einer – tatsächlich erstaunlichen – Zusammenarbeit mit Wittmann entstanden, die vor allem auf einer guten Kommunikation beruhte und die ermöglichte, Prototypen allein auf der Basis der Aquarelle Steven Holls zu produzieren. So entstand auch der schwarze *Lendensessel*, ein klassischer Freischwinger, der überall im Hotel zum Einsatz kommt. Technische Herausforderungen waren die Lampen wie die *Frog-Lamp* im Bar-Bereich (das Pendant dazu befindet sich im Spa-Bereich) und die *Spider-Lamp* im Restaurant aus lackiertem, wassergestrahltem Schwarzblech. Zwischen Hotel und Besucherzentrum liegt der verbindende Weg in Form des *Wein.Kunstgartens*, eines inszenierten landschaftlichen, man könnte sagen: Psychogramms, versteckt im Weingarten: Ein Weg, der in Stationen den Winzer und seine Gefühle und Gedanken bei der täglichen Arbeit thematisiert.[10]

9 E-Mail-Korrespondenz mit Christian Wassmann, Dezember 2006

10 Auch der *Wein.Kunstgarten* entstand im Rahmen des Kunstprogramms *Festival der Gärten – Kamptal 2006*

neighboring town of Etsdorf) or the *Peanuts-Couch* in the spa area were added. 'The fine, expensive combinations of materials—furniture made of dark wood and black leather, thick carpeting—enter into a dialogue with the rough surfaces of the building and assure a feeling of comfort,' says Christian Wassmann who was responsible for the design of the furniture.[9] Beds, upholstered furniture and chairs, were developed in collaboration with Wittmann. This collaboration was indeed astonishing and was based primarily on good communication that made it possible to produce prototypes on the basis of Steven Holl's watercolors alone. This was also the way in which the black *Lumbar-Chair*, a classic cantilevered chair that is used throughout the hotel, was created. The lamps such as the *Frog-Lamp* in the bar (there is a pendant in the spa area) and the *Spider-Lamp* in the restaurant made of painted, water-blasted black sheet metal represented real technical challenges.

Between the hotel and visitors' center there is a connecting path in the form of the *Wein.Kunstgarten*, a psychogramm, so to speak, that is presented in the landscape and hidden in the vineyards: a path that thematically addresses the stages of a winegrower's life and his or her feelings and thoughts in daily work.[10] The poetic interpretation of these thoughts is realized in the form of *pocket gardens*, according to the Graz landscape planners ko a la. These are subtle designs that take into account the linearity of the rows of vines but also incorporate foreign materials in order to highlight the special qualities of the place by means of contrast.

9 Email correspondence with Christian Wassmann in December 2006

10 The *Wein.Kunstgarten* was also created in the framework of the art program *Festival der Gärten – Kamptal 2006*.

...the primarily glass three-story building stood there glowing, standing out like a U.F.O., set amid an expensive parking lot and muddy fields of fledgling vines.

...glühend stand das groß-teils aus Glas bestehende, dreistöckige Gebäude da, nicht unähnlich einem U.F.O., mitten drin zwischen großem Parkplatz und schlammigen Weingärten mit jungen Weinstöcken.

New York Times, December 4, 2005

Blick auf das Hotel
View of the hotel

Hotel Eingangsseite,
Ansicht von Norden
Hotel on the entrance side,
view from the north

Lobby mit Sofa (Entwurf: Steven
Holl)
Lobby with sofa (design: Steven
Holl)

Hotelflur mit Lichtschlitzen in
Form der Kellerröhren
Hotel lobby with light slits in the
form of cellar vaults

‚Holl Bar' mit *Frog-Lamp*
'Holl Bar' with *Frog-Lamp*

Spa-Bereich mit *Peanuts-Liegen* und der in den Fußboden integrierten *Frog-Lamp*
Spa area with *Peanuts-Couch* and the *Frog-Lamp* integrated into the floor

Die poetische Interpretation dieser Gedanken realisiert sich in der Form von Gärten, so die Grazer Landschaftsplaner ko a la. Es sind subtile Gestaltungen, die die Linearität der Rebzeilen achtet, jedoch ortsfremde Materialien miteinbezieht, um die Besonderheiten des Ortes im Kontrast hervorzuholen.

Vor dem Eingang zum Besucherzentrum noch einmal eine, hier bewusst gesetzte, kongeniale Gegensätzlichkeit des Landstrichs: Zusammengesetzt aus Fundamentsteinen alter Kampbrücken bildet die Skulptur *Kellergasse* von Franz Xaver Ölzant das raumgreifende Gegenüber des Silberwürfels. Hier kann man sich schon die Frage stellen, wer denn nun den bedrohlicheren Teil darstellt? Nach wie vor der *Silberwürfel*, der ja einst und oft mit außerirdischen, unsanft gelandeten Gebilden verglichen wurde? ‚Mit seiner Facettierung und matt geschliffenen Oberfläche ändert sich die Erscheinung des Gebäudes beim Umschreiten und je nach Sonnenstand‘, schwärmt Wassmann vom norwegischen Marinealuminium der Fassade.[11] Das heißt, er passt sich an, er nimmt Anteil am Tagesablauf und an den Jahreszeiten, ist also schon weit mehr ein freundlicher Einheimischer denn ein bedrohlicher Alien. Und tatsächlich, je weiter die Zeit fortschreitet, verwächst er zusehends mit den umgebenden Weinreben.

Im Inneren des Solitärs dann der freie, lichtdurchflutete Raum, um den sich das Programm mit Vinothek, Shop und Café gruppiert. Wieder, wie beim Hotel, selektive Fensterausschnitte, die die Korkwand aufbrechen und ausgesuchte Sequenzen der Umgebung freigeben. Im Unterschied zum Hotel ist das Möbel-

11 E-Mail-Korrespondenz mit Christian Wassmann, Dezember 2006

In front of the entrance to the visitors' center there is, once again, a brilliant and conscious use of contrast with elements typical of the region. Franz Xaver Ölzant's sculpture *Kellergasse* made up of foundation stones from old bridges over the River Kamp is a counterpart of the silver cube that intervenes in space. Here one can ask oneself which one is the more threatening? Is it still the *silver cube* that has often been compared with an extraterrestrial form that has landed awkwardly? 'Through its faceting and matt-polished surface as one walks around the building its appearance changes according to the position of the sun,' says Wassmann enthusing about the Norwegian marine aluminum of the façade.[11] That is to say it adapts itself, takes part in the changes during the course of the day and the season and is thus far more like a friendly native than a threatening alien. And in fact, with the passage of time it increasingly grows together with the surrounding vines.

Inside, the free-standing building is an open light-flooded space around which the program with vinothek, shop and café is grouped. Again, as in the hotel, selective window cut-outs break open the cork wall to reveal chosen sequences of the surroundings. In contrast to the hotel here, due to its function, the furniture program is more reduced and severe. But here, too, there is a mix of designs from Holl's office with additional pieces (such as Arne Jacobsen's classic *Ant*). The basic notion for the furniture—round formal idiom, light-colored wood, here augmented by the wave form as the basis of the design—was conceived in a

11 Email correspondence with Christian Wassmann, December 2006

programm funktional bedingt reduzierter und strenger gehalten. Aber auch hier ein Mix von Entwürfen aus dem Büro Holl und zusätzlichen Teilen (wie dem Stuhlklassiker *Ameise* von Arne Jacobsen). Der Grundstock der Möbel – runde Formensprache, helles Buchenholz, hier ergänzt durch die Wellenform als Grundlage des Entwurfs – ist im modularen Möbelprogramm für die Studentenzimmer der Simmons Hall am MIT in Cambridge, USA, gelegt worden, an dem das Büro Holl kurz zuvor gearbeitet hatte.

Letzter Abschnitt: Die *Kellerwelt*. Vorbei an den Bullaugen des Pools abwärts in Richtung Eingangstor mit seinen verschlüsselten Zeichen, die von den Gesetzmäßigkeiten, Unberechenbarkeiten sowie Unergründlichkeiten des jährlichen Prozesses der Weinwerdung erzählen. Dann taucht man ein in die Tiefen der unterirdischen Stadt, in eine Welt, in der Traum und Wirklichkeit ineinander fließen, und in der die Frage, was ist hier nun Inszenierung oder reale Kellerwelt, stille Begleiterin ist. In eine Welt der konzentrierten sinnlichen Erlebnisse.

Für die Dichte an Erlebnisqualitäten ist auf der einen Seite die Dramaturgie der Inszenierung verantwortlich, die sich nicht der Limitierung eines eng gefassten, erzählenden Kerns unterwirft, sondern die mit einer inhaltlichen Vielfalt das Thema auffächert: Gegenwärtiges wird Historischem gegenübergestellt, Alltägliches aus der Winzerwelt wird mit den mystisch-kultischen Qualitäten der Weinwerdung komplementiert, und historische Längsschnitte werden durch punktuelle Querschnitte anschaulich vertieft. Auf der anderen Seite legt aber auch die Vielfalt

modular furniture program for the student rooms of Simmons Hall at M.I.T. in Cambridge, U.S.A., which Holl's office had worked on a short time previously. The last section: the *cellar world*. Past the porthole windows of the pool in the direction of the entrance door with its coded symbols that tell of the laws, unpredictabilities and unfathomable aspects of the cyclical process of making wine. Then one plunges into the depths of the underground city, into a world in which dream and reality flow together, where the question what is just presentation, what is the real cellar world is a silent companion. Into a world of concentrated sensual experiences.

On the one hand, the dense experience is the result of the dramaturgy that is not limited by a narrowly defined narrative core, but that expands the theme through a diversity of contents. The contemporary is contrasted with the historical, everyday aspects from the world of the winegrower are complemented by the cultic, mystical qualities of the process through which wine is made and historical longitudinal sections are demonstrably deepened by punctual cross-sections. On the other hand, the variety of narrative forms employed—simulation, reconstruction, and mystification—deposit additional different layers of experience in the cellar labyrinth.

Entry into the wine world is shaped by the decisive final event of the winegrower's year, which either makes all the winegrower's earlier efforts fruitless or brings them to their fulminant final point: the fermentation. 'In autumn after the wine

Heimo Zobernig, Skulptur *Ohne Titel* am Käferberg bei Langenlois
Ohne Titel (Untitled), sculpture by Heimo Zobernig on Käferberg, near Langenlois

Detail *Wein.Kunstgarten*
Detail of the *Wein.Kunstgarten*

Installation im *Wein.Kunstgarten*
Installation in the *Wein.Kunstgarten*

F. X. Ölzant, Skulptur *Kellergasse*
vor dem Besucherzentrum
Kellergasse (Cellar Lane), sculpture by F. X. Ölzant, in front of
the visitors' center

an angewandten Erzählformen – Simulation, Rekonstruktion, Mystifikation – zusätzliche unterschiedliche Erlebnisschichten in das Kellerlabyrinth.

Den Einstieg in die Weinwelt prägt das entscheidende, finale Ereignis eines Winzerjahres, das all die vorangegangene Mühe des Winzers entweder zunichte machen oder zu einem fulminanten Endpunkt bringen kann: Die Gärung.

‚Im Herbst nach der Weinlese, nach einem langen Jahr Arbeit, konzentriert sich in wenigen Wochen alles auf den turbulenten Prozess der Gärung. In dieser Zeit, mit den letzten richtigen Entscheidungen, kann der Wein zum Kultobjekt werden', so erklärt Karl Steininger, was hier in einer spektakulären, multimedialen Inszenierung aus Film, Ton und Wasser in einem simulierten Gärprozess stattfindet.[12] Die Besucher, mittendrin im Gärtank, erleben den Prozess bis zu dem Punkt, an dem Bacchus den jungen Wein dem Winzer schenkt. ‚Der erste Schluck vom jungen Wein ist der spannendste Moment in unserem Jahr, aber auch der schönste. Aber dann muss der Wein ruhen', so Winzer Steininger.[13]

Das Ruhen des Weins nachempfinden kann man in den anschließenden dunklen, kühlen Kellergängen mit ihrem uralten Gewölbe und dem so typischen Geruch aus Keller und Wein. Alte Geräte, Werkzeuge und historische Filme vermitteln Fakten und Legenden zur Geschichte des Weinbaus und erklären den langen Prozess von der Arbeit im Weingarten bis hin zur fachkundigen Lagerung des Weins in den Kellergängen. Gleichzeitig wird bei jedem Schritt die aktuelle Nutzung der Keller präsent, wie die schweren Holzfässer, die in den Gängen gelagerten Weinflaschen

[12] Laut Gespräch mit Karl Steininger, Oktober 2006

[13] Ibid.

harvest, after a long year of work, in just a few weeks everything is concentrated on the turbulent process of fermentation. In this period, with the last correct decisions, wine can become a cult object,' says Karl Steininger, explaining what happens here in a simulated fermentation process that takes the form of a spectacular multimedia presentation made up of film, sound and water.[12] The visitors—actually inside the fermentation tank—experience the process to the point at which Bacchus gives the new wine to the winegrower. 'The first sip of new wine is the most exciting moment in our year, but also the most beautiful. But then the wine must rest,' says Steininger.[13]

Visitors can experience something of the way in which the wine must rest in the adjoining dark, cool, cellar passageways with their ancient vaults and typical smell of basement spaces and wine. Old appliances, tools and historic films convey facts and tell legends about the history of winegrowing and explain the long process from the work in the vineyards to the specialised storage of wine in the cellar passageways. At the same time the current use of the cellar is present at every step, such as the heavy wooden barrels, the wine bottles stored in the corridors and the riddling racks filled with bottles of sparkling wine. Also directly and immediately present is the loess, the centuries-old foundation of the underground town and the basis of the regional wine culture.

The *Zehnerhaus* is integrated in the ensemble of the cellar world in a presentation that provides an exemplary cultural and historical snapshot. The typical

[12] According to a conversation with Karl Steininger in October 2006

[13] Ibid.

und die mit Sektflaschen gefüllten Rüttelpulte zeigen. Unmittelbar gegenwärtig auch der Löss, das Fundament der unterirdischen Stadt und Basis der regionalen Weinkultur.

Ins Ensemble der Kellerwelt ist das *Zehnerhaus* integriert, das mit seiner Inszenierung eine exemplarische kulturhistorische Momentaufnahme darstellt. Das typische Ackerbürgerhaus mit spätmittelalterlichem Kern und Barockfassade wurde umfassend renoviert und gibt Einblick in einen typischen Tag der Familie Loiskandl. Man schreibt das Jahr 1924, die Zeit kurz nach dem Ersten Weltkrieg, als das Land sich vom tiefen Einschnitt des Krieges erst wieder regenerieren musste. Die Familie lebt vom Weinbau und einer bescheidenen Viehzucht. Nicht ungemütlich ist es in der warmen Küche, wo das Feuer im Ofen knistert und ein großer Laib Brot rastet und in der hellen Stube mit dem Herrgottswinkel und der Pfeifensammlung von Vater Loiskandl. Eine volle Vorratskammer und die Essigflaschen im Vorraum (aus eigener Produktion für den Verkauf bereitstehend) zeugen davon, dass die Familie Selbstversorger war. Wache Augen können hier im Hause Loiskandl eine Unzahl an authentischen Gegenständen des Lebens um 1924 entdecken. So auch in der hauseigenen Werkstatt und der Schusterwerkstatt im Hoftrakt nebenan.

Auf eine ganz andere Alltäglichkeit trifft man mitten im historischen Kellerlabyrinth mit der Produktionsstätte der Familie Steininger. Je nach Jahreszeit kann man hier von der Pressung der Trauben über die Gärung bis zur Flaschenabfüllung

Ackerbürgerhaus with its late mediaeval core and Baroque façade has been comprehensively restored and offers an insight into a typical day of the Loiskandl family. It takes a day in 1924, the time after the First World War when the land still had to regenerate from the effects of war. The family lived from winegrowing and modest animal husbandry. It is not uncomfortable in the warm kitchen, where the fire crackles in the stove and a large loaf of bread rests, and also in the bright parlor with the crucifix in the corner and old Mr Loiskandl's pipe collection. A full pantry and the bottles of vinegar in the hall (home-made and waiting to be sold) show that the family could support itself. Sharp-eyed visitors can find innumerable authentic items from life as it was led in 1924 in the Loiskandl house, and also in the workshop and cobbler's workshop in the adjoining courtyard wing.

In the historic cellar labyrinth one encounters a very different kind of everyday world in the form of the Steininger family's wine production facility. According to the time of year visitors can follow different aspects of the production process from the pressing of the grapes to fermentation to filling the bottles. The tall stainless steel tanks are in this case real, computer-operated high technology products in which wine truly ferments. Everything is within touching distance. Generally, Karl Steininger himself is to be found here and with his profound explanations can almost make the winegrower's life—the dream and the reality—into the part of the presented narrative. Since autumn 2003 his business

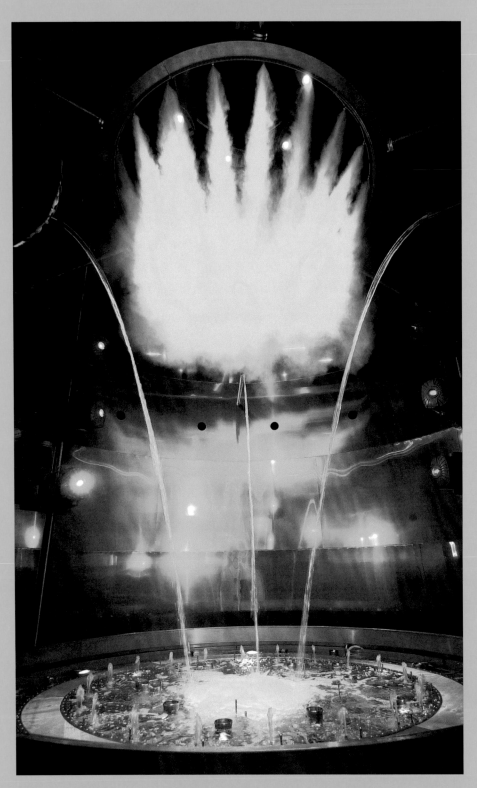

Gärdom: multimediale
Simulation des Gärprozesses
Fermentation tank: multimedia
simulation of the fermentation
process

Gebetsmühlen
Prayer wheels

Musikalische Darbietung im
Festsaal bei der ersten *Loisiarte*
Musical performance in the
festival hall at the first *Loisiarte*
festival

Rechts: Blick zum Pool und zum
Eingang ins Café
Right: View towards pool and
entrance at café

Mein Dank gilt den zahlreichen
Personen, die mich mit den
nötigen Informationen versorgt
haben. Allen voran Tuula und
Gerhard Nidetzky für ihre groß-
zügige Unterstützung sowie ihre
stete Begeisterung, ebenso
Dietmar Steiner für die Gespräche
und sein Vertrauen; weiters
Brigitte und Karl Steininger, Winzer
und Mitinitiatoren des LOISIUM;
Brigitte Schlögl, Geschäftsführung
des LOISIUM Besucherzentrums,
und Ulrike Lauter, Assistenz
Geschäftsführung LOISIUM Hotel;
Otto J. Steiner von Steiner Sarnen
Schweiz; Architekten Christian
Wassmann, Irene Ott-Reinisch,
Franz Sam, Bernd Leopold und
Andreas Gattermann; Veronika
Oberwalder und Robert Kutscha.

den Produktionsvorgang nachvollziehen. Die hohen Edelstahltanks sind in diesem Fall reale computergesteuerte, hochtechnische Anfertigungen, in denen der Wein nun wahrhaft gärt. Alles zum Angreifen nahe. Meist ist Karl Steininger selbst hier zu finden und versteht es, mit seinen profunden Erklärungen diese Winzerrealität – Traum und Wirklichkeit – beinahe wieder zur inszenierten Erzählung werden zu lassen. Seit Herbst 2003 ist sein Betrieb nun Teil der LOISIUM Weinwelt. Seitdem lebt er mit der Kellerwelt und ihren BesucherInnen gut und gerne.

Im letzten Teil der Kellergänge wird der Wein von seinen regionalen Bezügen gelöst und die jahrhundertealte Verehrung angestimmt, die ihm seit der Kultivierung der ersten Weinrebe in mythischer Vorzeit zukommt. Eng verbunden mit den rhythmischen Gesetzmäßigkeiten der Natur, wie dem Wechsel des Wetters und der Mondwanderung, nahm er bald Platz in der Götterwelt und der christlichen Ikonologie. Stahlskulpturen wie Gebetsmühlen, ein Pendel und die tanzende ‚Weinberggoas‘ stehen bereit, von den Besuchern in rhythmische Schwingungen versetzt zu werden, um ihre magischen Schatten ins Halbdunkel der Kellergänge zu werfen. Im weiten, tonnengewölbten Raum des Festsaals schlussendlich trifft sich bei kulturellen Veranstaltungen wie der *Loisiarte* – ein eigens für das LOISIUM entwickeltes Festival für Musik und Literatur – Vergangenheit und Gegenwart, um den für das Gesamtprojekt LOISIUM so typischen Dialog zwischen Alt und Neu lebendig zu halten.

has formed part of the LOISIUM wine world. Since then he has lived happily and gladly with the cellar world and its visitors.

In the final part of the cellar corridors the wine is detached from its regional references and the centuries-old veneration begins that wine has enjoyed since the cultivation of the first grape vines in the mists of mythical, prehistoric times. Closely connected with the rhythmical laws of nature, like the changes of the weather and the phases of the moon, it soon occupied a place in the world of the gods and in Christian iconology. Steel sculptures like prayer wheels, a pendulum and the dancing *Weinberggoas* (wineyard goat) stand ready to be set oscillating typically by visitors and to cast their magical shadows into the semi-darkness of the cellar passageways. In the wide, barrel-vaulted space of the festival hall, where cultural events such as the *Loisiarte*—a festival of music and literature developed specially for the LOISIUM—are held, the past and the present meet to keep alive the dialogue between old and new that is so typical of the LOISIUM project as a whole.

My thanks are due to the numerous people who provided me with
the necessary information. Above
all thanks to Tuula and Gerhard
Nidetzky for their generous support and their unfailing enthusiasm,
also to Dietmar Steiner for the
conversations and his confidence;
to Brigitte and Karl Steininger,
winegrowers and co initiators of
the LOISIUM; Brigitte Schlögl,
manager of the LOISIUM visitors'
center, and Ulrike Lauter, assistent
manager of the LOISIUM Hotel;
Otto J. Steiner from Steiner
Sarnen Schweiz; architects
Christian Wassmann, Irene Ott-
Reinisch, Franz Sam, Bernd
Leopold and Andreas Gattermann;
Veronika Oberwalder and Robert
Kutscha.

Wie ein Meteorit ist das futuristische Bauwerk in die Weinberge des niederösterreichischen Kamptals eingeschlagen.

This futuristic building has struck the vineyards of the Lower Austrian Kamp valley like a meteorite.
Frankfurter Allgemeine Zeitung,
30. September 2004

Innenansicht Besucherzentrum
Interior view of the visitors' center

Vorhergehende Doppelseite:
Blick vom Hotel auf Langenlois
mit dem Besucherzentrum im
Vordergrund
Previous pages: View of
Langenlois from the hotel,
showing the visitors' center in
the foreground

Links: Detail Ostfassade
Left: Detail east elevation

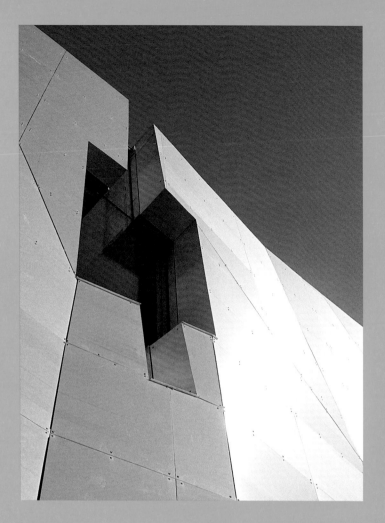

Vorhergehende Doppelseite:
Blick vom Pool in Richtung
Eingang Kellerwelt
Previous pages: View from the
pool towards the entrance to the
cellar world

Besucherzentrum, Detail
Westfassade
Visitors' center, detail west
elevation

Nächste Doppelseite: Hotel,
Blick auf den Westflügel mit
Restaurant und Wein-Bibliothek
Following pages: Hotel, view of
the west wing, showing the
restaurant and the wine library

Verbindungsgang zwischen Kellerwelt und Besucherzentrum,
darüber der Pool mit Bullaugen
Tunnel connecting cellar world
and visitors' center, above lies
the pool with portholes

Links: Blick auf die Aluminium-
fassade des Hotels, im Hintergrund das Besucherzentrum
Left: View of the aluminum
façade of the hotel, in the
background the visitors' center

Nordseite des Hotels mit
auskragenden Obergeschossen
Hotel north side, showing the
protruding upper floors

Innenhof des Hotels mit Pool
Inner courtyard and pool

Lobby mit Kiesler-Sitzecke
Lobby with furniture designed
by Frederick Kiesler

Hotelzimmer: im Vordergrund
Sofa mit Stoffmuster in Form der
Kellerröhren
Hotel room: in the foreground a
sofa displaying a fabric with the
cellar vault pattern

Solche Bauherren hat man einmal und dann träumt man das ganze Leben davon.

You have this type of client once and then dream the rest of your life about having someone like them again.

Irene Ott-Reinisch, Oktober 2006

Lobby mit Stiegenaufgang in die Obergeschosse
Lobby with staircase to the upper floors

im gespräch mit steven holl
in conversation with steven holl

Es war ein Augenblick sofortiger Inspiration

GH Sie haben einmal betont, dass es für Sie schon immer interessant war, sich mit den beiden Extremen von Uralt und Ultramodern in einem einzigen Projekt intensiv auseinanderzusetzen. Insofern muss doch das Langenloiser Projekt für Sie ideal gewesen sein. Welchen Eindruck hatten Sie, als Sie das Bauland im März 2001 zum ersten Mal sahen? Was waren Ihre ersten Ideen?

SH Diese Zeichnung hier ist die Schlüsselskizze [s. S. 75]. Sie entstand in der Nacht, nachdem ich erstmals vor Ort war. Das war am 11. Juni 2001. Die Bauherren Tuula und Gerhard Nidetzky führten mich durch die alten Weinkeller, und ich sah eine wunderschöne Karte dieser merkwürdigen Morphologie, der Gestalt dieser Weinkeller. Ich hatte sofort die Idee zu dieser verrückten Sprache – beinahe eine Art neues Formenalphabet, das das Alte mit dem Neuen verbinden sollte. Mit dem Durchschneiden der unterirdischen Formen durch einen simplen Würfel [dem Wein- oder Besucherzentrum] werden die Keller zu Lichtquellen, während sie selbst dunkel bleiben. Das Hotel wiederum entstand dann als Reaktion darauf oder in Umkehrung dazu. Das Konzept verlief also vom Keller zum Weinzentrum bis zum Hotel. Eines ist *under the ground*, eines *in the ground* und eines *above the ground*. Es war ein Augenblick intuitiven Denkens und sofortiger Inspiration.

Merkwürdig, ich hätte gedacht, dies hier wäre die erste Skizze für das Langenloiser Projekt gewesen [s. S. 74].

It Was a Moment of Immediate Inspiration

GH You once pointed out that you have always been interested in probing the two extremes of the ancient and the ultra modern in one site. With this challenge in mind, the Langenlois project must have been the ideal project for you. How did you feel about the site when visiting it for the first time in March 2001? What were your first ideas?

SH Actually, this drawing is a key drawing [see page 75]. It was made in the middle of the night after I first saw the site. On 6/11/01 I went to the site for the first time. The clients, Tuula and Gerhard Nidetzky, took me through the old vine vaults, and I saw a wonderful map of this strange morphology, the shapes of these vaults. I immediately had this idea of making this almost weird language, almost a kind of new alphabet of shapes, the link between the old and the new. By cutting a simple cube of space [the wine or visitors' center] via these subterranean shapes they become the source of the light, whereas in the vaults they are dark. And then making the hotel may be in response as well as in an inversion. So it goes from the cellar to the wine center to the hotel. And one is *under the ground*, one is *in the ground* and one is *above the ground*. It was a moment of immediate thinking, of immediate inspiration.

Strange, I would have thought this was the first sketch you drew for the Langenlois project [see page 74].

Ja, da haben Sie recht. Aber diese, mit 14. März 2001 datierte, zeigt nur die drei Teile der Gewölbe [s. S. 74]. Man erkennt zwar schon die alte Morphologie, den Kubus des Weinzentrums und das Hotel. Die Gebäude haben aber noch keine artikulierte Form. Außerdem fehlt in dieser Skizze die Idee des *under the ground*, *in the ground* und *above the ground*. Die mit 11. Juni 2001 datierte Zeichnung zeigt hingegen die Grundidee [s. S. 75]. Ich brauchte dafür also drei Monate. Das heißt, dass mir erst jetzt, wo ich hier mit Ihnen sitze und rede, auffällt, dass ich mich an etwas anderes erinnere, als das, was wirklich geschah (lacht).

Wie ging es weiter, nachdem Sie die endgültige Idee skizziert hatten?

Von den Aquarellen gehen wir immer zu den Modellen über, wovon wir immer viele anfertigen. Das kann schnell gehen, aber auch eine Zeitlang in Anspruch nehmen. Die Entwicklung des Hotels dauerte sehr lange; wir haben unzählige Modelle, die belegen, wie wir damit gekämpft haben. Das Weinzentrum gelang viel schneller. Das liegt daran, dass das Hotel komplexer ist – das Programm war vielfältiger, und ich wollte unbedingt, dass die Hotelzimmer über den öffentlich zugänglichen Räumen schweben. Ich glaube, dass viele Architekten und Architektinnen, die Ansprüche haben, kämpfen müssen. Die Balance zwischen Grundidee, Form und Komposition ist eben ein Kampf; es dauert lange, bis alles zusammenpasst. Es wurden schon viele Gebäude auf der Welt gebaut, aber nur wenige besitzen diese besondere Intensität. Und geht man der Sache auf den Grund, war meistens jemand dafür verantwortlich, der kämpfen musste – so wie ich.

Oh, you are right. But this one, dated 03/14/01, only shows the three parts of the vaults [see page 74]. There already is the old morphology, the cube of the wine center and the hotel, which is all part of the program. But the buildings don't have articulated forms. And this sketch does not contain the idea of *the under*, *the in* and *the over*. But the sketch, dated 6/11/01, is the one that became the idea [see page 75]. So it took me three months to develop the idea. This means, sitting here and talking to you, I realize that over the years, one's idea of what happened becomes different from what actually happened. (laughs)

How did you proceed after you had sketched out the final idea?

From the watercolors we always go to the models, and we always make many models. This process can be quick, but sometimes it takes a long time. The hotel took a very long time to develop; we have a lot of models that show how we struggled trying to make it. The wine center was much quicker. This was because the hotel was more complex—there were a lot of different programs and I wanted the rooms to float over the public space. I think that many architects who are really searching for something—they have to struggle. This balance of program, form and composition is a struggle; it takes a long time to get everything to come together. There are a lot of buildings built in the world and some of them have this intensity. And usually, if you go deep into where they came from, they came from someone struggling, like myself.

I would strongly argue that both the wine center and the hotel are well

Steven Holl, Zeichnung, die die
Idee des ‚unter, in und über der
Erde' zeigt, 14. Juni 2003
Steven Holl, drawing showing
the idea of the 'under, in and
above the ground,' June 14, 2003

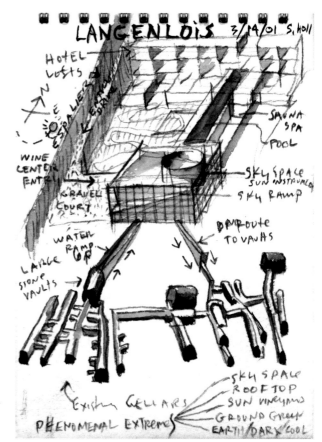

Steven Holl, Entwurfszeichnung
der Gesamtanlage, 14. März 2001
Steven Holl, design drawing for
the entire complex, March 14, 2001

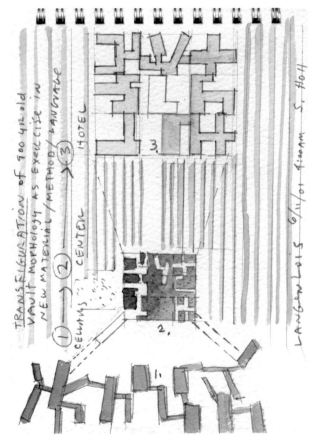

Steven Holl, Entwurfszeichnung
der Gesamtanlage, 11. Juni 2001
Steven Holl, design drawing for
the entire complex, June 11, 2001

Ich würde meinen, dass sowohl das Besucherzentrum als auch das Hotel gut in die Umgebung integriert sind. Steht diese Homogenität in Zusammenhang mit Ihrem Entwurfsprozess, im Zuge dessen Sie eingehend die Besonderheiten des Ortes aufspüren?

Es freut mich, das zu hören. Und ja, am 11. Juni 2001 hatten wir ein Konzept: Die Verbindung von etwas Modernem mit etwas sehr Altem. Doch das war zugleich auch ein Schock für mich, denn während ich diese Skizzen zeichnete, dachte ich, sie sollten nicht an alte Architektur erinnern, weil das dem Alten gegenüber zu respektlos wäre. Ich muss etwas aus dem 21. Jahrhundert machen! Als ich dann die Entwürfe erstmals in Langenlois präsentierte, stellte ich klar, dass meine Bauten, selbst wenn sie zu den Gewölbeformen darunter Bezug nahmen, etwas Neues seien und in komplementärem Kontrast stünden. Der Bürgermeister meinte in der Besprechung: ‚Wir bauen dieses Weinzentrum und auch das Hotel.' Ich hatte keine Ahnung, dass dies die Baubewilligung war. Allerdings bedeutete das auch, dass ich das Gebäude später nicht verschieben konnte, weil die Behörden auf Grundlage meiner ursprünglichen Zeichnung einen Widmungsplan erstellt hatten, der auf den Raum für die Neubauten zugeschnitten war – und so konnte ich nicht mehr zurück.

Könnten wir zur Frage der Homogenität zurückkommen?

Ja, ich denke, die hängt wirklich mit dem Gewölbesystem zusammen, und auch damit, dass es sich um kompakte Geometrien handelt. Zum Beispiel hat dieser

integrated into their surrounding landscape. Could one relate this homogeneity to the design process in which you profoundly explore the specific qualities of any site you work on?

First, this is nice to hear. And yes, on 6/11/01 we had a concept. We had a theme: the link between something modern and something very old. But it was also a shock to me, because when I made these sketches I thought, I should not make them recall this old architecture; that would be too disrespectful of the old. I have to make something of the twentyfirst century. So when I presented this at Langenlois for the first time, I said quite clearly that, even if this has a relationship to the shapes of the vaults underneath, this is something new and in complementary contrast. The mayor was in this meeting and said: 'We are going to build this wine center and the hotel as well.' And little did I know that that was a building permit. But that meant that I could not move the building later on, because based on my original drawing they issued a zoning envelope that fits that new space for the new buildings and I could no longer go outside of it.

Could we return to the question of homogeneity?

Yes, I think it really is related to the vault system, then to the fact that these are compact geometries. There is for example the fact that this void equals this solid (the hotel court geometry equals the wine center volume), and the fact that they are related on the surface of the earth under, in and over. So I think the possibility of these connections in four different ways allows for the architecture

Leerraum dasselbe Volumen wie diese Festform (die Geometrie des Hotelvorplatzes gleicht dem Umriss des Weinzentrums). Außerdem hängen sie unterirdisch, ebenerdig und überirdisch zusammen. Ich glaube, diese vier Assoziationsmöglichkeiten machen die Architektur zu etwas Neuem und Andersartigem, während sie zugleich im Boden und in der Geschichte des Orts verwurzelt bleibt. Das ist diese tiefe Verbindung zu dem, das ich aus dem Bauplatz herausgelesen habe. Die Bauarbeiter, Bauunternehmer, Konstrukteure – alle verstanden diese Idee sofort. Sie akzeptierten sie, obwohl sie niemals zuvor so ein Gebäude errichtet hatten.

Wie Sie bereits erklärt haben, basiert die erste Skizze zum Langenloiser Projekt auf den drei typologischen Elementen unter, in und über der Erde. Wieso taucht dieses Motiv, das sie schon früh in ihrem Werk verwendet haben, hier in diesem Projekt wieder auf?

Es handelt sich nicht wirklich um eine Typologie, sondern um den Begriff der Erdoberfläche, und dass jede Architektur in Beziehung dazu steht: Sie kann sich nur unterhalb, innerhalb oder oberhalb davon befinden. Es geht um Erdbezogenheit und nicht um ein Motiv wie z.B. eine Geometrie oder eine Form.

Es handelt sich also um einen universellen Zugang?

Ich habe diese Dreiteilung 1986 zum ersten Mal in einer Art Manifest in meinem Buch *Anchoring* in Bezug auf das Mailänder Projekt Porta Vittoria erwähnt. Anstatt einen persönlichen Stil zu entwickeln, den ich auf den unterschiedlichen Bauorten wiederhole, versuche ich an jedem Ort eine neue Architektur. Das

to be something quite new and quite different, but it is grounded in the earth and in the history of the place. It is the deep connection to something that I read out of the site. The workers on the site, the builders and the constructors—they all understood this idea immediately. They accepted it, even though they had never built a building like this before.

As you have explained, the first sketch of the Langenlois project was based on the three typological parts under, in, and over. How would you explain that this motif, which you applied early on in your work, reappears here in this project?

It is not really a typology, but rather a zero ground thinking about the earth and buildings. It is this notion of the surface of the earth and that all architecture is in relation to this surface: it only can be under, in or over. This is an idea of relativity to the earth not really a motif as it could be any geometry or form.

So, it is a sort of universal approach?

The first time I established this as a kind of manifesto was in 1986 in my book *Anchoring* in the Milan Porta Vittoria project. So, rather than having a style that I carry and try to put down on all these different sites, I try to have a new architecture for each site. I try not to have a personal style. This makes it difficult for any client, because I am unpredictable, I am dangerous for the clients. They don't know what concept they will get. It is very hard for me to be selected through a short-list. It is easier for me to win a competition as a way of getting a project.

Architekt Steven Holl
vor dem Hotel
The architect Steven Holl
in front of the hotel

Modellstudien zum Hotel
Model studies of the hotel

Südseite Besucherzentrum
South side of the visitors' center

macht es natürlich für die Bauherren schwer, weil ich unberechenbar und damit
für sie gefährlich bin. Sie wissen nicht, welches Konzept sie vorgelegt bekommen
werden. Gibt es einen zweiten Durchgang, komme ich deswegen selten zum Zug.
Für mich ist es leichter ein Projekt durch einen Wettbewerb zu gewinnen.

**Mir ist ihr Vergleich zwischen der geometrischen Anlage der Rebzeilen und dem
,städtischen Raster' aufgefallen. In Langenlois sind wir auf dem Land…**

Aber die Landschaft ist nicht ländlich! Sie ist von Menschen gemacht. Die Geometrie der Stadt formt den Raum. Wenn man das Raster einer Stadt durchwandert
und den Himmel betrachtet, so ist der Raum des Himmels in ein geometrisches
Muster zergliedert. Und wenn man die Zeilen eines Weinbergs durchwandert, ist
der Raum des Himmels gleichermaßen durch das geometrische Muster des Weingartens gegliedert. Es gibt eine Beziehung zwischen unserer Raumerfahrung und
geometrischer Strenge, ob sich nun ein Raster, eine fixe Geometrie oder parallele
Raumstreifen zwischen Gebäuden oder zwischen Grünfluchten befinden. Hier
in Langenlois handelt es sich definitiv um eine künstliche Art der Raumerfahrung,
die sehr schön ist. Es gibt nichts Schöneres als vollreife Weingärten. Es war
interessant, dass die alte Stadt, das Weinzentrum und das Hotel in dieses strenge
Verhältnis einbezogen werden konnten. Deswegen müssen die neu gepflanzten
Rebenzeilen zwischen dem Weinzentrum und dem Hotel genau so laufen, wie sie
heute laufen, um diese Elemente zu verbinden. Es ist auch sehr wichtig, dass die
neuen Reben so nahe wie möglich an das Hotel gepflanzt wurden, sodass man

I have always been intrigued by your comparison of the geometric spacing of
the vineyard rows with 'the grid of the city.' Because in Langenlois, we are out
there in this rural landscape…

But this landscape is not rural. It is man-made. The geometry of the city forms
space. As you walk through the city grid and look at the sky, the space of the sky
is cut in a geometric pattern. And equally, when you walk between the rows of
the vineyard, the space of the sky is cut through the geometric pattern of the
vineyards.

There is this relationship between the way we experience space and the geometric rigor of something. It does not matter if the grid or rigid geometry or
the parallel strips of space are between buildings or between green rows. It is
definitely a man-made kind of spatial experience here in Langenlois, which is
very beautiful. When the vineyards are full, there is nothing more beautiful. And
it was very interesting that the old city, the wine center and the hotel could enter
into this rigorous relationship. Thus the newly planted lines of vines between
the wine center and the hotel have to run in exactly the way they are today
in order to connect these parts. It was also very important that the new vines be
planted as close to the edge of the hotel as possible, so when you are in the café,
restaurant or spa, you can see these vines coming right up to the glass. That is
a unique experience.

You have always kept close ties to Europe, starting with your early studies in

sie vom Café, vom Restaurant oder vom Spa-Bereich aus bis direkt ans Fenster kommen sieht. Das ist ein einzigartiges Erlebnis.

Sie haben immer eine enge Beziehung zu Europa gehalten, beginnend mit ihren frühen Studien in Rom, dann mit mehreren Wettbewerben und nicht zuletzt mit dem Kiasma Museum in Helsinki. Was bedeutete es für Sie, in Österreich zu bauen?

Es war ein sehr schönes Erlebnis. Die heimischen Architekten Irene [Ott-Reinisch] und Franz [Sam] waren extrem wichtig. Sie waren für all die mühsame Arbeit verantwortlich, für die ganzen Detailpläne. Ich habe nur die Skizzen angefertigt. Nur so konnte ich arbeiten, denn ich kannte die österreichischen Gepflogenheiten nicht. Ich glaube, ein Grund für das Gelingen des Projekts war die hohe Fachkenntnis der Beiden. Das machte das Projekt so besonders – alle Involvierten investierten viel Energie. Von meiner Seite war der Projektleiter Christian Wassmann extrem engagiert. Aber auch die Handwerker und alle anderen Beteiligten waren sehr gut. Ich würde gerne noch etwas in Österreich bauen. Ich schätze diese Achtung vor handwerklichem Können und auch die harte Arbeitsmoral der Leute.

Wie gut kannten Sie vor dem Projekt den österreichischen Wein?

Ich wusste nur wenig darüber. Ich kannte den Grünen Veltliner, diesen herrlichen, trockenen Wein. Doch wusste ich nichts über seine lange Geschichte, den Variantenreichtum und seine Qualität. Es gibt 60 verschiedene Arten Grünen Veltliner! Und diese Umsicht, mit der die Winzer für diese Weinvielfalt sorgen! Sie sind extrem tüchtig. Das ist wunderbar.

Rome, then with several competitions, and last but not least with the Kiasma Museum in Helsinki. What did it mean for you to build in Austria?

It was a very good experience. The local architects, Irene [Ott-Reinisch] and Franz [Sam], became very important. They did all the hard work, all the detailing. I only did the sketches. And that is how I could work, because I did not understand the Austrian method. And I think one reason why we achieved what we did was that they knew exactly what was important; they had all the necessary expertise. This is what made the project so special—all the people involved gave a lot of energy. Also from my side, Christian Wassmann, the project architect, gave his all. All the craftsmen and all the other people working on the project were very good. I would love to build something else in Austria. I like the sense of craftsmanship and the hard-working nature of the people.

How well did you know Austrian wine before?

I knew a little about it. I knew the Grüner Veltliner, this wonderful, dry special wine. But I didn't realize the depth, the variety and the quality. There are 60 different varieties of Grüner Veltliner—I had never imagined that there could be so many varieties! And all the care the winegrowers take to ensure the variety of the wines. They are so involved. It is wonderful.

Let's turn to the design of the furniture. How could you create such a coherent atmosphere even though the furniture is composed of several individually designed pieces?

Kommen wir zum Design der Möbel. Wie gelang es Ihnen, eine so einheitliche Atmosphäre zu erzeugen, obwohl die Einrichtung aus mehreren individuell gestalteten Möbeln besteht?

Bei allen Möbeln ging ich von derselben Vorstellung aus. Die Sofabezüge zeigen die Morphologie der Reben. Sie wurden aus Webstoffen hergestellt, schwarz und gelb. Und auch die Sessel beziehen sich auf die Reben, wie man an diesen geschwungenen Linien erkennt. Der Entwurf der Sessel stammt aber auch aus einer Zeit in meinem Leben, in der ich starke Rückenschmerzen hatte. Ich wollte ihn *Loisium-Lendensessel* nennen. Als Ausgangspunkt für den Entwurf nahm ich diesen ‚Lendendruck am Rücken‘. Und er funktioniert auch als normaler Speisesessel. Die Lichtelemente, die Türschnallen – alle Formen beziehen sich auf die Kellergewölbe. Es ist wie bei einem Musikstück, in dem sich ein verbindendes Thema durch alles hindurchzieht. Ich schätze es sehr, dass die Nidetzkys all dies unterstützten. Noch einmal, das macht das Projekt so speziell: Alle Beteiligten strengten sich aufs Äußerste an, damit wir trotz des engen Zeitrahmens fertig werden konnten. In einer Idealwelt jedoch hätte ich mir ein Jahr mehr erbeten.

Nehmen wir das doch als letzte Frage: Was hätten Sie geändert, wenn Sie noch ein Jahr zur Verfügung gehabt hätten?

Wer weiß, ich hätte vielleicht mehr an der Einrichtung gefeilt, an den Proportionen, an Formen und Farben. Aber letztlich kommt diese Vorstellung, ein Jahr mehr haben zu wollen, davon, dass man als Architekt immer den Prozess auskosten will.[*]

* New York, Januar 2007

Mein Dank gilt neben Steven Holl auch David van der Leer und Hollyamber Kennedy (beide Steven Holl Architects) für ihre großzügige Unterstützung mit Material und Informationen, insbesondere während meines New York Aufenthalts.

They all came out of the same set of concerns. The bed has a bedspread with the morphology of the vines. They made that out of woven material, black and yellow. And the chairs are related to the vines too, as you can see from these lines that are curving around. But the design of this chair also originated during a particular time in my life when my back was hurting very badly. I wanted to call it the *Loisium Lumbar Chair*. So I took the position of this 'lumbar-push-on-the-back' as the beginning of the design. And it works as a regular dining chair.

The light fixtures, the door handles—all these shapes were related to the vaults. It is like a piece of music, where there is some thread of a theme that connects things. I was very happy that the Nidetzkys would allow us to do this. They were very supportive. Again, that was what made the project so special: everybody made such a huge effort to make this work though we had such a tight deadline. Actually, in an ideal world, I would have asked for one more year.

So let's make this the final question: What would you have changed if you had had another year?

Who knows, I might have worked on the furniture more, on proportions, on shapes and colors. But this idea of one more year results from the fact that as an architect, there is always a desire to enjoy the process.[*]

*New York, January 2007

My thanks are due to Steven Holl as well as to David van der Leer und Hollyamber Kennedy (both Steven Holl Architects) for their generous support with material and information, especially during my stay at their New York office.

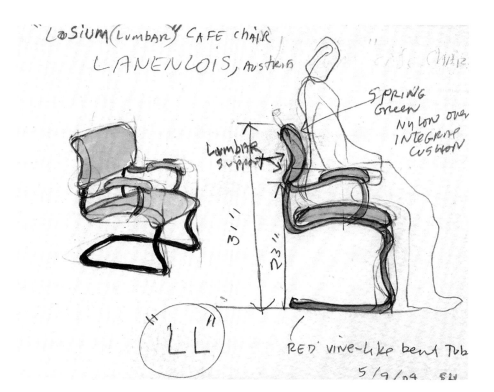

Steven Holl, Entwurfszeichnung
für den *Loisium-Lendensessel*

Steven Holl, design drawing for
the *Loisium Lumbar Chair*

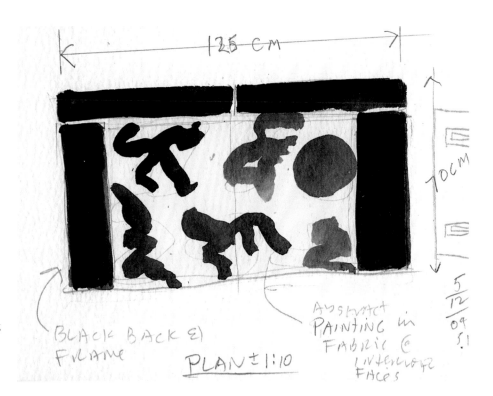

Steven Holl, Entwurfszeichnung
für das Sofa der Gästezimmer

Steven Holl, design drawing
for the sofa in the guest room

.im gespräch mit otto j. steiner
.in conversation with otto j. steiner

Ständig eine Sprache entwickeln, die es noch nicht gibt ...

GH Sie kommen gerade von der Übergabe eines neuen Projekts an einen Kunden: dem *Zermattlantis* in der Schweiz. Dieses Projekt ist bereits das sechste, das 2006 eröffnet wurde, und ein Hinweis auf Ihre bilderbuchartige Laufbahn: Angefangen von Ihren Ausstellungen für die Hergiswiler Glasfabrik Anfang 1990, über den Botanischen Garten im Schloss Meran, bis zur Inszenierung für die Riedel Glasfabrik in Tirol 1998 verdichten sich Ihre Aufträge seit 2000. Im Moment befinden Sie sich gerade in Endverhandlungen mit einem bulgarischen Schigebiet. Wie erklären Sie sich diesen Erfolg? Hat sich ihre Strategie des Fünf-Punkte-Programms – Vision, Konzeptphase, Planung, Realisation und Nachbetreuung – bewährt? Inwiefern mussten Sie mit der Zunahme und mit dem größeren Umfang der Projekte Ihre Arbeitsweise nachjustieren?

OJS Wir haben ein transparentes Rezept, wie wir arbeiten und wie wir an Projekte herangehen. Das ist durchaus an unsere Kunden vermittelbar. Das setzt sich einfach durch. Dabei handelt es sich nicht um einen individuellen, sondern um einen kollektiven Leistungsdruck, den wir generieren. Und vieles hängt von glücklichen Zufällen und guten Konstellationen ab, für die man aber auch kämpfen muss. Prinzipiell sind diese fünf Punkte, die wir vor längerer Zeit entwickelt haben, noch immer für unseren Arbeitsprozess sehr wichtig. Dann gibt es noch andere Erkenntnisse, wie die Gewaltentrennung von ,was' und ,wie' innerhalb der

Constantly Develop a Language Which Does Not Yet Exist ...

GH You have just returned from handing over to a client one of your new projects, the *Zermattlantis* in Switzerland. This project is already the sixth which has been opened in 2006 and is the latest addition to an already impressive resumé: starting with your exhibitions for Hergiswiler glassworks at the beginning of 1990; the Botanical Gardens in Meran Castle; the multimedia staging of the Riedel glassworks in Tyrol in 1998; and since 2000, an increasing number of commissions. At the moment, you are in the final negotiations for a project in a Bulgarian ski area. How would you explain your success? Has the strategy of your five-point program—vision, conceptual phase, planning, realization and post-consultation—proven itself? How, if at all, have you had to change your way of working, taking the increased number and size of projects into account?

OJS We have a transparent formula for the way we work and how we approach projects. This formula can also be communicated to our clients. It simply establishes itself. Yet it is not about the individual but rather the collective pressure to perform which we generate. And much has to do with lucky coincidences and agreeable alignments, for which one does have to struggle. In principle the five points which we developed quite a long time ago are still very important for our work process. Then there are other insights, such as the separation of powers between the 'what' and 'how' within the production strategy, and the vital

Produktionsstrategie, die wichtige Trennung zwischen dem Inhalt und seiner Umsetzung. Zunächst müssen wir wissen, was wir inhaltlich erreichen wollen. Dabei helfen uns ‚Erkenntnisträger' (Wissenschafter, Spezialisten, Museumsleute etc.). Erst wenn diese Absichtserklärung, diese Botschaft, formuliert ist, sind wir als Autoren an der Reihe mit dem ‚wie' der Darstellung. Danach wird alles in den Dienst dieser Absichtserklärung gestellt. Dabei eröffnen wir anfänglich einen großen Ideenpool, wo alles erlaubt, wo das Absurde gesucht ist.

Sie sprechen jetzt von Schritt Eins der Vision?

Ja. In diesem Prozess werden viele unbrauchbare Ideen in einer Art Geistreinigung weggeworfen. Es ist schwierig, immer neue Gedanken zu haben, aber diese Schwierigkeit systematisieren wir. Und bei der Beschäftigung mit dem ‚wie', kommt immer stärker die ‚Frage der Matrix' zum Tragen, an der ich theoretisch sehr intensiv arbeite. Das sind Fragen, wie die Besucher sich orientieren, in die Tiefe tauchen, daraus wieder hervorkommen.

Das heißt, man kann bei Ihrer Arbeit von einer Akkumulierung an Erfahrungen sprechen, die von Projekt zu Projekt weitergetragen werden?

Ja, gerade im Moment wachsen wir extrem in der Erfahrung, im Know-how, in der Sicherheit. Aber unsere Erfahrungen werden nicht eins zu eins auf das nächste Projekt übertragen. Kopieren ist nicht unser Weg und einfaches Kopieren funktioniert auch nicht. Wir müssen ständig eine Sprache entwickeln, die es noch nicht gibt.

Wieweit sind amerikanische Entwicklungen auf dem Gebiet der Erlebniswelten

differentiation between the content and its execution. First we must know what we want to achieve in terms of content. Here we are aided by 'insight bearers' such as scientists, specialists, people active in museums, and so forth. Only after this statement of intent, this message, has been formulated is it our turn as authors to express the 'how' of the presentation. After this, everything is done in the name of this statement of intent, whereby at the beginning we open up a huge pool of ideas where everything is allowed and where even the absurd is sought after.

You are now speaking of the vision, the first point in the program?

Yes. In this process many unusable ideas are disposed of in a kind of mental cleansing. It is difficult to always have new thoughts, but we have systemized this difficulty. And by occupying ourselves with the question of 'how,' the 'matrix issue' on which I work intensively on a theoretical level becomes increasingly prominent. These are questions such as how the visitors will orient themselves, dive into the depths, and then emerge again.

This means that in your work, one can speak of an accumulation of experiences which are carried over from project to project?

Yes—at the moment we are expanding immensely in terms of experience, know-how, and certainty. But our experiences cannot be carried over one-to-one to the next project. Imitation is not our style and simple imitation doesn't function in any case. We must constantly develop a language which does not yet exist.

Im Innenhof des *Zehnerhauses*
Inner courtyard of the *Zehnerhaus*

Vorraum des *Zehnerhauses*
Hall of the *Zehnerhaus*

Take the proffered earphones and blanket, descend into a deep, labyrinthine cellar, and enter a grown-up Disneyland for wine lovers.

Nehmen Sie sich den Kopfhörer und eine Decke, steigen Sie hinunter in den tiefen, labyrinthischen Keller, und betreten Sie ein Erwachsenen-Disneyland für Weinliebhaber.
Boston Sunday Globe, September 11, 2005

Sektpulte im Kellerabschnitt der Familie Steininger
Rack for sparkling wine in the section of the cellar belonging to the Steininger family

für Sie interessant? Wieweit spielt das globale Phänomen der Disneyfizierung für Sie eine Rolle?

Wir sind natürlich ständig darüber informiert, was weltweit an Entwicklungen auf diesem Gebiet läuft. Die Arbeiten Walt Disneys kenne ich gut und sie interessieren mich sehr. Dabei ist es nicht wichtig, dass mir das alles gefallen muss. Viel gelernt haben wir sicherlich von der Erzählstrategie der Amerikaner: Die Besucher erst einmal ankommen lassen, sie zu begrüßen und an der Hand zu nehmen, sie dann aber zum Fliegen und Genießen zu entlassen, um sie zuletzt wieder abzuholen. Ganz wichtig ist auch, dass die Besucher eine Devotionalie oder eigentlich in diesem Zusammenhang passender: eine ‚Emotionalie' mit nach Hause nehmen. Wenn das gelingt, dann gibt das eine gute Geschichte. In diesem Bereich haben wir von anderen Attraktionen viel gelernt. Wir haben aber noch eine andere Quelle der Anregung, das ist die Gegenwartskunst, vor allem die Aktionskunst. Vieles davon verwenden wir als Zitat. Denn wir machen ja nicht Kunst, wir machen Anwendung, wir machen Erzählung. Das ist unser oberstes Prinzip: Wir wollen eine Geschichte erzählen und wir haben gute Geschichten.

Wieso war das Projekt der Langenloiser Kellerwelt für Sie interessant? Als Bau auf der grünen Wiese widerspricht die Aufgabenstellung ja Ihrem eigentlichen Interesse. Sie interessieren sich ja vor allem für die Neuinterpretation von Orten mit gewachsenen Strukturen. Was war die Faszination dabei?

Wenn ein Auftraggeber kommt und es keinen offensichtlichen Grund gibt, ihn

To what extent do American developments in the area of theme parks interest you? And to what extent does the global phenomenon of 'Disneyfication' play a role?

Naturally we are up-to-date on global developments in this area. I know Walt Disney's work well and am very interested in it. It's not important for me to like everything. We have certainly learned a lot from the American narrative strategy: first allow the visitors to arrive; greet them, take them by the hand; then release them to fly and enjoy, ultimately picking them up again. It is also vital for visitors to take some type of souvenir home with them or, what would be even more appropriate in this setting, a type of emotional souvenir. If this happens, then we have a good story. We have learned much from other attractions in this respect. But we have another source of stimulation, namely contemporary art and above all performance art. We have quoted much from them. Because we are not making art, but rather applications; we are telling stories. This is our primary principle: we want to tell a story—and we have good stories.

Why did the Langenlois cellar world project interest you? A building on a greenfield site is not something you would usually be interested in doing. You are most interested in new interpretations of places with existing structures. What was your fascination with the project?

If clients approach us and there is no obvious reason to reject them, than we take them on. And if the clients turn out to be tolerant and ready to accept what we think is right, then we are very happy to work with them, because there are

abzulehnen, dann nehmen wir ihn. Und wenn sich der Auftraggeber dann noch als tolerant herausstellt und bereit ist, das zu akzeptieren, was wir für richtig finden, dann arbeiten wir sehr gerne mit ihm. Dann gibt es keinen uneffizienten Streit. Und das war hier der Fall. Wir haben sehr schnell gespürt, dass es sich um ein großes Thema handelt, aber auch, dass es touristisch in einem Niemandsland liegen wird, an dem der große Touristenstrom der Wachau vorbeizieht. Und generell arbeiten wir sehr gerne an Strukturen, die der Umgebung dienen, auch wenn es Neuland ist. Das LOISIUM, ich meine da das Gesamtprojekt, das war klar, wird für die Region eine bedeutende Rolle einnehmen. Als Beispiel: Ich war gestern bei Eco-Plus, der Niederösterreichischen Förderstelle. Wenn man dort sieht, wie wenige der zahlreichen Projekte vom Boden abheben oder bald wieder notlanden werden, dann nimmt das LOISIUM schon eine Sonderstellung ein.

Was war die Vision bei der Gestaltung der Langenloiser Kellerwelt? Welche Geschichten und Erzählstrategien kamen zum Einsatz?

Zuerst stellte sich die Grundfrage, was wir mit den ‚Fingern im Löss' machen könnten. Dank dem Grundwasser liegen die einzelnen Gänge auf derselben Höhe und waren bereits auch vereinzelt miteinander verbunden. Durch neu gebaute Stichtunnels konnten wir ein zusammenhängendes Labyrinth herstellen.

Die zweite Frage war: Wo steigen wir ein? Die engen Platzverhältnisse am Stadtplatz und in der Walterstraße zwangen uns, einen komplett neuen Eingang zu suchen. Der endgültige Platz des Besucherzentrums wurde auch in Hinblick auf

no inefficient conflicts. And that was the case here. We sensed very quickly that this was a major topic, but also that it would lie in a type of tourism no-man's land, far off the beaten path of the Wachau tourists. Generally we enjoy working on structures which serve the environment, even when it is virgin soil. The LOISIUM, and here I mean the overall project, was clearly going to play a major role in the region. Let me give you an example: yesterday I visited Eco-Plus, Lower Austria's business agency. There you can see just how few of the numerous planned projects actually get off the ground; and if they do, how many of them have to make an emergency landing. When you consider this, the LOISIUM occupies a very special place indeed.

What was your vision in the design of the Langenlois cellar world? Which stories and narrative strategies were put to use?

First there was the essential question of what we could do with the 'fingers in the loess.' Due to the groundwater the separate passageways lie at the same level and were already connected to each other individually. By building new connecting tunnels we were able to construct a seamless labyrinth.

The second question was: where do we enter? The limited space available on the Stadtplatz and the Walterstrasse forced us to look for a completely new entrance. The final location of the visitors center was selected on the basis of parking spot availability. And then there was the question of dramaturgy: because of the many different topics and diverse locations we decided on one specific editing

genügend Parkplätze ausgewählt. Und nun stellte sich die Frage nach der Drama-turgie: Aufgrund der vielen Themen und unterschiedlichen Standorte entschieden wir uns für eine Cut-Technik und verschiedene Erzählformate. Der Gärdom, das *Zehnerhaus*, Steiningers Keller und der Festsaal verlaufen zwar in einer losen Timeline, leben aber von den überraschenden Darstellungen und der Vielfalt der Erlebnisformen. Die Keller kündigen die jeweils kommende Attraktion an: Vor dem Zehnerhaus haben wir alte Kellerutensilien inszeniert, vor Steiningers Keller verläuft der längste neue Kellergang, und vor dem Festsaal stehen die mystischen Kunstwerke von Hugo Schär. Der Spaziergang durch die Keller vermittelt anhand der unterschiedlichen Darstellungsformen einen vielfältigen Einblick in die Produk-tion und das Leben der Weinbauern. Dank der einzelnen Attraktionen kommen die Besucher immer wieder in wärmere Gefilde und ,erfrieren' uns nicht. Und dank dem langen Tunnel am Ende des Kellerrundgangs steht man überraschenderweise wieder im Besucherzentrum, dem ursprünglichen Ausgangsort. Dies ist vielleicht auch ein Mittel der Verwirrung, um einen dem Betrunkensein nicht unähnlichen Zustand zu erreichen. All dies haben wir bereits in unserem ersten Papier festgelegt – auch wenn sich das Projekt im Laufe der Produktion verdichtet und verändert hat.

An welchen Punkten in der Kellerwelt wird denn die Steiner-Sarn'sche Philosophie am besten spürbar?

Das ist auf alle Fälle das *Zehnerhaus*, das sehr gut funktioniert und das wir sehr mögen. Hier liegt auch unsere Stärke, das Erzählen von Geschichten. Und generell

technique and various narrative forms. The fermentation tank, the *Zehnerhaus*, Steininger's cellar and the festival hall do indeed run on a loose timeline, but live from the surprising staging and the multiplicity of experiences. The cellars announce each coming attraction: in front of the *Zehnerhaus* we dramatized the old cellar utensils; the longest new cellar passageway runs in front of Steininger's cellar; and Hugo Schär's mystic works of art are placed in front of the festival hall. Through its various forms of presentation, a walk through the cellar conveys multifaceted insights into the production of wine and the lives of winegrowers. To see the individual attractions the visitor must return frequently to the warmer climes, thereby escaping the chill periodically. And thanks to the long tunnel at the end of the cellar tour, one once again is suddenly standing in the visitors center, the original point of departure. This may perhaps be a means to confuse, or to arouse in the visitor a feeling similar to drunkenness. All these things were laid down in our first paper—even though the project saw changes and consoli-dations within the course of production.

At which points in the cellar world is the Steiner-Sarnian philosophy most palpable?

Most definitely with the *Zehnerhaus*, which functions well and which we like very much. Here is our strength: telling stories; and in general, the radicalism that the presentation was able to maintain despite certain changes that were made.

Which experiences were you able to incorporate into the Langelois cellar world

die Radikalität, die die Inszenierung trotz mancher Änderungen behalten konnte.

Welche Erfahrungen konnten Sie von Ihrer Inszenierung für die Riedel Glasfabrik in Kufstein in die Kellerwelt von Langenlois einfließen lassen?

Die Arbeit für Riedel bildete eine Art Vorwissen. Aber wir mussten dann noch viel tiefer in die Welt des Weins eintauchen. Dabei hatten wir gute Führer wie Pfarrer Denk, Karl Steininger und viele andere. Das ist eigentlich auch das Schönste an unserer Arbeit, das sind Privilegien. Allerdings ist man danach gefordert, dass man auch etwas Gutes abgibt.

Konnten sie bei Ihren Projekten in Österreich so etwas wie ein ,typisch österreichisches' Publikum feststellen?

Ja natürlich gibt es immer ein ortspezifisches Publikum. Jeder Ort zieht andere Gruppen von Menschen an. Und mit unseren Antworten können wir diese Segmente erweitern, vielleicht sogar komplett neue Gruppen anziehen. Österreich-spezifisch scheint mir eine starke Deutschland-Orientiertheit zu sein. Die Erwartungen, die Späßchen, die Ansprache, die gemeinsamen Bilder, die Lebensgefühle, das Tempo sind uns da bekannter. Aber ab einer gewissen Stufe sprechen wir nicht mehr in Orts- oder Landessprachen, irgendwann müssen wir tiefere Erkenntnisse über das Leben, seine Tiefen und Höhen anklingen lassen. Es ist eine Spekulation, und manchmal gelingt es, eine Schwingung von ganz unterschiedlichen Herkunftsmentalitäten zu erwischen. Wir versuchen es immer, schaffen es aber nicht immer. Wenn es gelingt, entsteht eine innere Dankbarkeit gegenüber diesem Glück.*

* Langenlois, Dezember 2006

from your multimedia staging of the Riedel glassworks in Kufstein?

The work for Riedel formed a kind of pre-consciousness. But we then had to dive much deeper into the world of wine. For that, we had excellent guides such as Father Denk, Karl Steininger, and many others. This is actually the nicest thing about our work, the privileges. However, we are then challenged to produce something good from them.

Have you been able to divine a kind of 'typically Austrian' audience in the course of your projects in Austria?

Yes of course, there is always an audience unique to a given place. Each place attracts a different group of people. With our answers, we were able to expand this segment and in fact even attract completely new groups. Specific to Austria—I sense a strong orientation toward Germany. The expectations, the jokes, the forms of address, the shared images, attitude toward living and the pace of life—these are more familiar to us. But beyond a certain level we no longer converse in regional or national languages; there comes a time when we have to allow deeper insights on life to resound, both its highs and its lows. It is speculation, but sometimes we manage to catch on to a vibe from a completely different source and mentality. We always try to feel the vibe, but don't always succeed. When we manage to do so, we feel a deep sense of inner gratitude for this lucky event.*

* Langenlois, December 2006

1

Neue Kellerröhre im Tagbau
errichtet
New open-pit cellar vault

2

Einbau des Gärdoms
Installation of fermentation tank

3

Blick in eine der alten
bestehenden Kellerröhren
View into one of the old existing
cellar vaults

4

Temporäre Abstützungen beim
Einbau des Produktionsbetriebs
der Familie Steininger
Temporary supports for the
installation of the production
business of the Steininger family

5

Neu errichtete Kellerröhre
Newly built cellar vault

6

Eingebauter Gärdom und Blick
auf das Besucherzentrum
Build-in fermentation tank and
view of visitors' center

7

Unterirdischer Verbindungsgang
kurz vor dem Betonieren der
Decke
Lower tunnel just before
pouring a concrete ceiling

8

Hof des *Zehnerhauses* während
den Renovierungsarbeiten
Court of *Zehnerhaus* during
renovation work

9

Renovierung des *Zehnerhauses*
Renovation of *Zehnerhaus*

1

4

7

2

3

5

6

8

9

1

1

Baugrube mit Fundament
Building pit with foundations

2

Blick zur Westseite mit Café-
Bereich und Seminarraum
West view with café area and
seminar room

3

Aufgang zur VIP-Terrasse
Access to VIP terrace

4

Fassadendetail mit Fenster-
konstruktion
Detail of façade with window
construction

5

Unterirdischer Verbindungsgang
Besucherzentrum – Kellerwelt
Lower tunnel connecting
visitors' center to cellar world

6

Bullauge im Verbindungsgang
Porthole in connecting tunnel

7

Fensteraussparungen der
Südfassade
Window recesses on southern
side

8

Assemblierung der Fassadenteile
in der Montagehalle
Assembly of façade panels in
assembly hall

9

Anbringung der Aluminium-
platten
Mounting of aluminum plates

4

7

2

3

5

6

8

9

1

Spa-Geschoss mit Hohlkehlen-
säulen
Spa area and fluted columns

2

Einbetonierung der *Frog-Lamp*
in die Decke des Spa-Bereichs
Concrete mounting of *Frog-Lamp*
in ceiling of spa area

3

Saunageschoss mit Hohlkehlen-
säulen
Sauna floor and fluted columns

4

Bewehrung der Decke über dem
Erdgeschoss
Reinforcement of first floor
ceiling

5

Wandlayout der Zimmerebenen
Wall layout of upper floors

6

Stiegenlauf von der Lobby in
die Obergeschosse
Staircase from lobby to upper
floors

7

Oberer elliptischer Teil der
Lobbystiege
Upper elliptical part of lobby
stairs

8

Dicke und dünne Säulen
(‚Bäume') tragen die zwei
auskragenden Zimmergeschosse
der Nordseite
Thick and thin columns ('trees')
supporting the protruding upper
floors on the northern side

9

Luftaufnahme Besucherzentrum
und Hotel
Aerial view of visitors' center
and hotel

1

4

7

2

3

5

6

8

9

Jeden Monat landet ein ‚Diamant' zeitgenössischer Architektur irgendwo auf unserem Planeten. Das Spektakel Architektur hat globale Dimensionen angenommen. Was medial vor zehn Jahren noch als vereinzelte Sensation gefeiert wurde, die seltene Realisierung eines Traums aus der Welt der Architektur-Avantgarde, ist zu einem geradezu alltäglichen Ereignis geworden.

Steven Holl gilt als Star-Architekt. Doch nicht als solcher wurde er für das LOISIUM-Projekt engagiert. Kein herbeigewünschter Bilbao-Effekt, kein mediales Marketingkonzept standen am Beginn der Planung. Steven Holls LOISIUM-Projekt ist vielmehr eine originäre und einzigartige Gesamtstrategie, ein heute bereits architekturgeschichtliches Landmark, wie es nur aus einer ‚altmodischen' Beziehung von engagierter Bauherrschaft und Architekten entstehen konnte. Das LOISIUM kann mit Fug und Recht als Sternstunde der Architekturgeschichte bezeichnet werden.

Eine gewagte Behauptung, der eine Begründung zu folgen hat. Dazu bedarf es einer Bestimmung der Situation, in der sich Architektur heute befindet. Die Geschichte beginnt 1980 mit der von Paolo Portoghesi kuratierten Architekturbiennale in Venedig, die gemeinhin als Höhepunkt der Postmoderne in der Architektur bezeichnet wird. Portoghesi konzipierte im Arsenal eine *strada novissima* und lud dazu zwanzig internationale Architekten ein, eine individuelle Hausfassade zu entwerfen, die dann von den Studios der Cinecittà realisiert wurde. Entscheidend war, dass diese zwanzig auserwählten Architekten erstmals als

nachwort
epilogue

Every month a 'diamond' of contemporary architecture arises somewhere on our planet. The spectacle of architecture has taken on global dimensions. What, ten years ago, was still being celebrated as an individual sensation, or the rare realization of a dream from the world of the architectural avantgarde, has today become an almost everyday event.

Steven Holl is regarded being a star architect. Yet it is not as such that he was engaged for the LOISIUM project. When planning started, there was no desire for a 'Bilbao effect' and no media-marketing concept. Rather, Steven Holl's LOISIUM project is an original and unique overall strategy, a landmark in architectural history even today, and it could only arise from an 'old-fashioned' relationship between committed clients and architects. LOISIUM might well be described with complete justification as a turning point in the history of architecture—a daring claim, but one that is based on good foundations.

However, it requires a definition of the situation in which architecture finds itself today. The story begins in 1980, with the architecture Biennale in Venice, curated by Paolo Portoghesi, which is generally described as having been a highlight of Postmodernism in architecture. At the Arsenal, Portoghesi designed a *strada novissima* and invited twenty international architects to design individual façades for the buildings, which were then implemented by Cinecittà studios. The decisive fact was that the twenty architects who were chosen were for the first time designated as 'star architects.' This was at a time when museum

‚Star-Architekten' bezeichnet wurden. Es war die Zeit, als weltweit der Museums-
bau zu boomen begann – Hans Holleins Museum Mönchengladbach und Renzo
Pianos und Richard Rogers' Centre Pompidou sind Meilensteine dieser Entwick-
lung und repräsentieren den Wechsel der Architektur in die Kulturindustrie.
Seit damals gibt es nicht mehr bloß bedeutende, einflussreiche oder avantgardis-
tische Architekten. Es gibt ‚Stars', Garanten für öffentlichen und medialen Erfolg.
Den Höhepunkt dieser Entwicklung bildete das 1997 eröffnete Guggenheim-
Museum in Bilbao. Es entsprach den neuen kulturindustriellen Bedingungen der
Architektur: dass ein Thomas Krens als Direktor der Guggenheim-Foundation
sich einen Frank O. Gehry als Star-Architekten für die Realisierung wünschen
konnte und dass ein dritter, nämlich die Stadt Bilbao und die Provinz des Basken-
landes, die Planungs-, Bau- und Folgekosten zu bezahlen hatte. Zweifellos
hat sich Bilbao, eine vordem sterbende Industriestadt, mit Gehrys Guggenheim
als Flaggschiff zu einer neuen Identität aufgeschwungen. Und seit damals spricht
man jedenfalls von einem ‚Bilbao-Effekt', dass ein einziges avantgardistisches
Architekturprojekt einer ganzen Region zu neuen Erfolgen des Tourismus und der
Attraktivität des Standorts zu verhelfen vermag.
Diesem ‚Bilbao-Effekt' folgend hat sich seit damals die Welle der attraktiven
‚Diamanten', die sich Investoren von Star-Architekten erwarten, über den ganzen
Erdball ausgebreitet. Immer wieder wurde damit spekuliert, dass die Signatur
eines Architekten allein schon genügt, um einem Projekt zum Erfolg zu verhelfen.

construction was beginning to boom all over the world—Hans Hollein's Museum
Mönchengladbach and Renzo Piano and Richard Rogers' Centre Pompidou are
milestones in this development and constitute architecture's changeover to the
arts industry.
Since then, there have no longer been architects who are simply important,
influential or avantgarde. There are 'stars,' guarantees for success in the public
eye and in the media. The high point of this development was the Guggenheim
Museum in Bilbao, which was opened in 1997. It corresponded to the new
conditions of architecture as determined by the arts industry: that a Thomas
Krens, as director of the Guggenheim Foundation, was able to obtain the services
of a Frank O. Gehry, as a star architect, to implement the building and that a
third party, namely the City of Bilbao, together with the Basque Province, had to
pay for the planning, construction and all the subsequent costs. There can be
no doubt that Bilbao, which had previously been a dying industrial city, was then
raised up and acquired a new identity, with Gehry's Guggenheim serving as
the flagship. At any rate, ever since then, one has spoken of the 'Bilbao effect,'
namely that a single avantgarde architectural project can help a whole region to
achieve new success in tourism and become a more attractive location.
Since that time, as a result of this 'Bilbao effect,' the wave of attractive 'diamonds'
which investors expect from star architects has expanded all over the globe. Time
and again it is speculated that simply the signature of an architect will suffice to

Doch nirgendwo stellte sich ein Bilbao vergleichbarer Erfolg ein, keine andere Stadt wurde durch einen Bau eines Star-Architekten gerettet. Es überrascht, dass dies nie jemand hinterfragt hat. Gewiss ist, dass die Bilbao folgenden ‚Diamanten' der diversen Stars zumindest für mediale Aufmerksamkeit sorgten, aber es war ihnen zumeist nur eine kurzzeitige Präsenz in den Medien beschieden, bis sie von der inzwischen inflationären Verbreitung weiterer spektakulärer Projekte wieder von der ‚Ökonomie der Aufmerksamkeit' verdrängt wurden.

Es wird also Zeit, sich von der medialen Aufmerksamkeit als Kriterium für die Bedeutung von Architektur langsam wieder abzuwenden, um sich mit den konkreten Bauten zu beschäftigen. Denn jenseits medialer Verbreitung gibt es einfach sehr gute und wichtige Architektur – auch von Star-Architekten. Dabei steht heute jeder Star-Architekt vor der Frage, wie er oder sie einen Auftraggeber einzuschätzen hat, und muss eine Auswahl treffen. Und in einem boomenden Begehren der Investoren nach Big Names der Architektur ist die Verführung groß. Aber auch die Enttäuschung der Architekten, wenn sie erkennen müssen, dass kein Interesse an Qualität besteht, sondern nur der Name gekauft werden soll.

Im Falle LOISIUM konnte Steven Holl schon im ersten Kontakt mit dieser Aufgabe davon überzeugt werden, dass er es nicht mit spekulativen ‚clients' zu tun hatte, sondern mit ‚patrons', die von ihm eine besondere architektonische Lösung erwarteten und diese auch in seinem Sinne begleiten und umsetzen würden. Dafür war am Beginn des Projekts eine vertrauensbildende Moderation ebenso

make a project successful. Yet nowhere has there been any success similar to that of Bilbao and no other city has been saved by a building designed by a star architect. It is surprising that no-one has questioned this. What is certain is that the 'diamonds' created by the various stars subsequent to Bilbao have at least attracted media attention, although they were usually only granted short-term media presence, lasting only until they were once again ousted from the 'economy of attention' by the now inflationary propagation of further spectacular projects.

It is therefore high time to gradually renounce media attention as a criterion for the significance of architecture, in order to occupy ourselves with the actual buildings. Beyond media propagation there is, quite simply, very good and important architecture—even by star architects. Every star architect is today faced with the question of how he or she should estimate a client and then has to make a choice. And the temptation is great as long as there is a boom in the investors' desire for the big names of architecture. Yet so is the disappointment of the architects, when they have to recognize that no-one is interested in quality, but simply in using their name for the purposes of selling.

In the case of LOISIUM, Steven Holl could be convinced, upon his first contact with the brief, that he was dealing not with speculative 'clients,' but with 'patrons,' who expected a special architectural solution from him and would also support him in implementing it. For this purpose, at the very beginning of the project,

notwendig wie lokale Kontaktarchitekten gefunden werden mussten, die in der üblichen Schere zwischen architektonischen Ideen und gegebenem Kostenrahmen über die notwendigen technischen und regional-spezifischen logistischen Kenntnisse verfügten, eine zunächst abstrakte architektonische Vision auch baulich umzusetzen. Franz Sam und Irene Ott-Reinisch gebührt dieses einmalige Verdienst, Steven Holls Vision in gebaute Realität übersetzt zu haben.

Heutzutage entsteht ein architektonisches Meisterwerk nur dann, wenn das Konzept des Architekten im begleitenden Vertrauen des Auftraggebers und in der engagierten Mitwirkung aller ausführend beteiligten Büros und Firmen verwirklicht werden kann. Da wird die große Welt der medialen Aufmerksamkeit wieder ganz klein und ganz persönlich. Und nur weil all diese Voraussetzungen vorhanden waren, konnte Steven Holl in Langenlois das LOISIUM mit seinem Eingangspavillon und dem Hotel als ein Meisterwerk der Architekturgeschichte realisieren.

confidence-building moderation was just as necessary as finding local contact architects who, despite being caught in the usual divide between architectural ideas and a given costs framework, had the necessary logistic and technical knowledge to be able to also implement an architectural vision that might at first seem rather abstract. All due credit goes to Franz Sam and Irene Ott-Reinisch for having provided the unique service of translating Steven Holl's vision into constructed reality.

Today, an architectural masterpiece only arises when the architect's concept can be implemented with the accompanying trust of the clients and with the committed collaboration of all the studios and companies involved. It is then that the big wide world of media attention becomes quite small and very personal. And only because all these requisite conditions were satisfied, was it possible for Steven Holl to achieve his LOISIUM in Langenlois, with its entrance pavilion and hotel, and in the process to create a masterpiece of architectural history.

Nächste Doppelseite: Restaurant *Vineyard*

Following pages: *Vineyard* restaurant

Initiatoren Besucherzentrum, inszenierte Keller und Hotel
Dkfm. Gerhard und Tuula Nidetzky, Karl und Brigitte Steininger
Erwin und Annemarie Haimerl

LOISIUM Besucherzentrum Loisiumallee 1, Langenlois, Österreich
Bauherr: Loisium Kellerwelt Betriebs GmbH & Co KG, Langenlois
Entwurfsarchitekt: Steven Holl Architects, Steven Holl in Zusammenarbeit mit
Solange Fabião, New York
Kontaktarchitekten: arge architekten, Irene Ott-Reinisch – Franz Sam, Wien
Projektleitung: Christian Wassmann, Steven Holl Architects, New York
Projektteam: New York: Martin Cox, Jason Frantzen, Brian Melcher, Olaf Schmidt;
Wien: Sabine Bassista, Klaus Gabriel, Karin Sam
Statik: Retter & Partner Ziviltechniker/Ing. Dieter Gausterer, Krems
Fassaden: Marine Aluminium/Heinrich Renner GmbH, Langenlois
Haustechnik: Altherm Engineering GmbH, Baden
Beleuchtung: Zumtobel Staff, Dornbirn
Möbel: Schmidingermodul, Schwarzenberg; Büro + Plan, Wien
Programm: Café, Vinothek, Shop, Seminarraum, Veranstaltungsbereiche, Büros
Grundstücksfläche: 3.635 m²
Nutzfläche: 1.280 m²
Bebaute Fläche: 660 m²
Umbauter Raum: 10.525 m³
Planungsbeginn: 2001
Bauzeit: Oktober 2002 – September 2003
Baukosten Besucherzentrum und Kellerwelt: 9,3 Mio EUR (kofinanziert durch
Regionalförderung des Landes Niederösterreich und EU-Fördermittel)

Inszenierte Keller LOISIUM Loisiumallee 1, Langenlois, Österreich
Künstlerische Leitung: Hugo Schär, Steiner Sarnen Schweiz (SSS)
Projektleitung: Niggi Stöcklin, SSS
Architektur: Marc Boog, SSS
Andreas Gattermann, Krems
Gestaltung Zehnerhaus: Roberto di Valentino, SSS
Licht- und Tontechnik: Matthias Krainer, Marc Metz, Fa. Werkplan, Karlsruhe
Planung Szenografie: Ute Schimmelpfenning, Michael Zeyfang,
Fa. m.o.l.i.t.o.r., Berlin
Musik: Rochus Keller, Schweiz
Bubbles Installation: Wolfgang Münch, Kioshi Furukawa, Karlsruhe

LOISIUM Hotel Loisiumallee 2, Langenlois, Österreich
Bauherr: Loisium Hotel Betriebs GmbH & Co KG, Langenlois
Entwurfsarchitekt: Steven Holl Architects, Steven Holl, New York
Kontaktarchitekten: arge architekten, Irene Ott-Reinisch – Franz Sam, Wien
Projektarchitekt: Christian Wassmann, Steven Holl Architects, New York

Initiators of Visitors' Center, Cellar World and Hotel
Gerhard and Tuula Nidetzky, Karl and Brigitte Steininger
Erwin and Annemarie Haimerl

LOISIUM Visitors' Center Loisiumallee 1, Langenlois, Austria
Client: Loisium Kellerwelt Betriebs GmbH & Co KG, Langenlois
Principal Architect: Steven Holl Architects, Steven Holl in collaboration with
Solange Fabião, New York
Local Architect: arge architekten, Irene Ott-Reinisch – Franz Sam, Vienna
Project Architect: Christian Wassmann, Steven Holl Architects, New York
Project Team: New York: Martin Cox, Jason Frantzen, Brian Melcher, Olaf Schmidt;
Vienna: Sabine Bassista, Klaus Gabriel, Karin Sam
Structural Engineer: Retter & Partner Ziviltechniker/Dieter Gausterer, Krems
Aluminum Façade: Marine Aluminum/Heinrich Renner GmbH, Langenlois
Mechanical Engineer: Altherm Engineering GmbH, Baden
Lighting: Zumtobel Staff, Dornbirn
Furniture: Schmidingermodul, Schwarzenberg; Büro + Plan, Vienna
Program: Café, vinotheque, shop, seminar room, event spaces, offices
Site area: 3,635 m^2
Floor area: 1,280 m^2
Built-up area: 660 m^2
Cubage: 10,525 m^3
Planning start: 2001
Construction phase: October 2002 – September 2003
Building costs for Visitors' Center and Cellar World: EUR 9.3 mn.; co-financed by
Eco Plus, the Business Agency for Lower Austria, and EU support programs

LOISIUM Cellar World Loisiumallee 1, Langenlois, Austria
Artistic Direction: Hugo Schär, Steiner Sarnen Schweiz
Project Manager: Niggi Stöcklin, Steiner Sarnen Schweiz
Architecture: Marc Boog, Steiner Sarnen Schweiz
Andreas Gattermann, Krems
Zehnerhaus Design: Roberto di Valentino, Steiner Sarnen Schweiz
Lighting and Acoustics: Matthias Krainer, Marc Metz, Werkplan, Karlsruhe
Scenography Planning: Ute Schimmelpfenning, Michael Zeyfang,
m.o.l.i.t.o.r., Berlin
Music: Rochus Keller, Switzerland
Bubbles Installation: Wolfgang Münch, Kioshi Furukawa, Karlsruhe

LOISIUM Hotel Loisiumallee 2, Langenlois, Austria
Client: Loisium Hotel Betriebs GmbH & Co KG, Langenlois
Principal Architect: Steven Holl Architects, Steven Holl, New York
Local Architect: arge architekten, Irene Ott-Reinisch – Franz Sam, Vienna
Project Architect: Christian Wassmann, Steven Holl Architects, New York

Projektteam: New York: Garrick Ambrose, Dominik Bachmann, Rodolfo Dias, Peter Englaender, Johan van Lierop, Chris McVoy, Ernest Ng, Olaf Schmidt, Brett Snyder, Irene Vogt

Wien: Bernd Leopold, Andreas Laimer, Karin Sam, Simone Ammersdorfer

Landschaftsplanung: ko a la – Robert Kutscha, Veronika Oberwalder, Graz; wagner/weitlaner, Wien

Statik: ARGE Hotel Loisium, Retter & Toms, Krems

Glasfassaden: Baumann Glas, Baumgartenberg

Alu-Fassaden: Heinrich Renner GmbH, Langenlois

Haustechnik: Altherm Engineering GmbH, Baden

Beleuchtung: Zumtobel Staff, Dornbirn

Polstermöbel: Franz Wittmann, Etsdorf am Kamp

Design Türgriffe: Solange Fabião, New York

Programm: 82 Hotelzimmer, Restaurant *Vineyard,* Lobby, Holl Bar, Wein Bibliothek mit Cigar-Lounge, AVEDA Wine Spa, beheiztes Outdoor Pool, Tagungsräume

Grundstücksfläche: 7.659 m^2

Nutzfläche: 6.712 m^2

Bebaute Fläche: 1.618 m^2

Umbauter Raum: 28.930 m^3

Planungsbeginn: März 2003

Bauzeit: Juni 2004 – September 2005

Baukosten: 14,8 Mio EUR (kofinanziert durch Regionalförderung des Landes Niederösterreich und EU-Fördermittel)

Project Team: New York: Garrick Ambrose, Dominik Bachmann, Rodolfo Dias, Peter Englaender, Johan van Lierop, Chris McVoy, Ernest Ng, Olaf Schmidt, Brett Snyder, Irene Vogt
Vienna: Bernd Leopold, Andreas Laimer, Karin Sam, Simone Ammersdorfer
Landscape Architects: ko a la – Robert Kutscha, Veronika Oberwalder, Graz; wagner/weitlaner, Vienna
Structural Engineer: ARGE Hotel Loisium, Retter & Toms, Krems
Glass Façade: Baumann Glas, Baumgartenberg
Aluminum Façade: Heinrich Renner GmbH, Langenlois
Mechanical Engineer: Altherm Engineering GmbH, Baden
Lighting: Zumtobel Staff, Dornbirn
Upholstered Furniture: Franz Wittmann, Etsdorf am Kamp
Door Handle Design: Solange Fabião, New York
Program: 82 hotel rooms, *Vineyard* restaurant, lobby, Holl Bar, wine library with cigar lounge, AVEDA Wine Spa, heated outdoor pool, conference rooms
Site area: 7,659 m^2
Floor area: 6,712 m^2
Built-up area: 1,618 m^2
Cubage: 28,930 m^3
Planning start: March 2003
Construction phase: June 2004 – September 2005
Building costs: EUR 14.8 mn.; co-financed by regional grant of the province of Lower Austria and EU support programs

Steven Holl Architects
459 W 31st Street, 11th floor
New York, N.Y. 1001, USA
www.stevenholl.com

Steven Holl geboren 1947 in Bremerton, Washington, USA. Architekturstudium an der University of Washington, 1970 Studienaufenthalt in Rom, 1976 Postgraduate-Studium an der Architectural Association in London; 1976 Gründung von SHA in New York City; seit 1989 Professur (seit 1981 Adjunct Professor) an der Columbia University Graduate School of Architecture and Planning, New York. Umfangreiche Lehrtätigkeit, zahlreiche Ausstellungen und Veröffentlichungen wie *Anchoring* (1989) und *Parallax* (2000). Zahlreiche Preise und Auszeichnungen (1998 Alvar Aalto Metal, 2002 National Design Award in Architecture, 2006 AIA Iowa Honor Award of Excellence).

Projekte (Auswahl): **1988** Haus in Martha's Vineyard, Mass. **1991** Texas Stretto Haus, Dallas, Texas **1991** Fukuoka Wohnkompex, Fukuoka, Japan **1997** St. Ignatius Kirche, Seattle, Washington **1998** Kiasma Museum of Contemporary Art, Helsinki, Finnland **1999** Y-Haus, Catskill Mountains, N.Y. **2000** Bürogebäude Sarphatistraat, Amsterdam, Niederlande **2001** Bellevue Art Museum, Bellevue, Washington **2002** MIT Simmons Hall, Cambridge, Mass. **2003** LOISIUM Besucherzentrum und **2005** LOISIUM Hotel, Langenlois, NÖ **2006** University of Iowa, Institut für Kunst und Kunstgeschichte, Iowa City, Iowa; Swiss Residence, Washington D.C.

In Planung: Nelson-Atkins Museum of Art, Erweiterung, Kansas City, Missouri; Linked Hybrid, Beijing, China.

Steven Holl was born in 1947 in Bremerton, Washington, U.S.A.; he graduated from the University of Washington and pursued architecture studies in Rome in 1970. In 1976 he joined the Architectural Association in London and established Steven Holl Architects in New York City. A tenured professor at Columbia University's Graduate School of Architecture and Planning since 1989, Holl has lectured and exhibited extensively and has published numerous texts including *Anchoring* (1989) and *Parallax* (2000). He has received numerous prizes and awards, including the Alvar Aalto Metal (1998), the National Design Award in Architecture (2002) and the 2006 AIA Iowa Honor Award of Excellence (2006). Select Projects: 1988 Martha's Vineyard House, Martha's Vineyard, Mass. 1991 Texas Stretto House, Dallas, Texas; Fukuoka Housing, Fukuoka, Japan 1997 Chapel of St. Ignatius, Seattle, Washington 1999 Y-House, Catskill Mountains, New York 1998 Kiasma Museum of Contemporary Art, Helsinki, Finland 2000 The Sarphatistraat Offices, Amsterdam, Netherlands 2001 Bellevue Art Museum, Seattle, Washington 2002 M.I.T. Simmons Hall, Cambridge, Mass. 2003 LOISIUM Visitors' Center and 2005 LOISIUM Hotel, Langenlois, Lower Austria 2006 School of Art and Art History, University of Iowa, Iowa City, Iowa; The Swiss Residence, Washington, D.C. Projects in planning: Nelson-Atkins Museum of Art (Extension), Kansas City, Missouri; Linked Hybrid, Beijing, China.

Sam/Ott-Reinisch
Franz-Josefs-Kai 45/1/6
1010 Wien/Vienna,
Österreich/Austria
www.samottreinisch.at

Franz Sam geboren 1956 in Tiefenfucha, NÖ. 1977–84 Studium der Architektur, TU Innsbruck, 1985–92 Projektleitung bei Coop Himmelb(l)au, seit 1992 eigenes Architekturbüro in Wien–Krems, 1994–2001 Hochschulassistent, Universität für angewandte Kunst in Wien, seit 1997 Konsulent der Baudirektion/Ortsbildpflege, Amt der NÖ Landesregierung, 1998–2002 Vizepräsident, Landeskammer der Architekten und Ingenieurkonsulenten für Wien, NÖ und Burgenland, seit 2002 Universität für angewandte Kunst und TU Innsbruck, seit 2005 Vorstandsvorsitzender ORTE Architekturnetzwerk, seit 2001 Zusammenarbeit mit Irene Ott-Reinisch.

Irene Ott-Reinisch geboren 1963 in Innsbruck, Tirol. 1982–91 Studium der Architektur, TU Innsbruck, 1992–95 Post-graduate-Studium: Technischer Umweltschutz, Universität für Bodenkultur und TU Wien, seit 2000 eigenes Architekturbüro in Wien, seit 2000 Konsulentin der Baudirektion/Ortsbildpflege, Amt der NÖ Landesregierung, seit 2005 Konsulentin der Austrian Development Agency für Bhutan, seit 2001 Zusammenarbeit mit Franz Sam.

Projekte in ARGE (Auswahl): **2001** Künstlerateliers und **2002** Fassadengestaltung Eyblfabrik, Krems **2001** Platzgestaltung Emmersdorf **2003** Ballsporthalle und Eissporthalle (in Bau) Landessportschule St. Pölten **2003** Wohnhaus Reither, Umbau, Krems **2005** Hochbehälter Reisperbachtal, Krems **2003** LOISIUM Besucherzentrum und **2005** LOISIUM Hotel, Langenlois **2006** Schulzentrum (in Bau), Waidhofen/Ybbs (alle NÖ). **In Planung:** Hotel Training and Management Training Institute, Thimphu, Bhutan.

Franz Sam born in 1956 in Tiefenfucha, Lower Austria. 1977–1984 studied at Innsbruck TU; 1985–1992 project management, Coop Himme(l)blau; since 1992 own office in Vienna/Krems; 1994–2001 assistant, University of Applied Arts Vienna; since 1997 consultant, Lower Austrian Provincial Government, Dept. of Construction/Town Preservation; 1998–2002 Vice-President, Regional Chamber of Architectural and Engineering Consultants for Vienna, Lower Austria, and Burgenland; since 2002 University of Applied Arts Vienna and Innsbruck TU; since 2005 Chairman, ORTE Architekturnetzwerk. Collaboration with Irene Ott-Reinisch since 2001.

Irene Ott-Reinisch born in Innsbruck, Tyrol in 1963. 1982–1991 studied at Innsbruck TU; 1992–1995 post-graduate studies in Technical Environmental Protection at the Vienna TU; since 2000 own office in Vienna and consultant to the Lower Austrian Provincial Government, Department of Construction/Town Preservation; since 2005 consultant to the Austrian Development Agency for Bhutan. Collaboration with Franz Sam since 2001.

Select Collaborative Projects: **2001** Artists' ateliers and **2002** Façade design, Eybl factory, Krems **2001** Design of public space, Emmersdorf **2003** Gymnasium and ice rink (under construction), State High School for Athletics, St. Pölten **2003** Renovation, Reither residence, Krems **2005** Water tower, Reisperbachtal **2003** LOISIUM Visitors' Center and **2005** LOISIUM Hotel, Langenlois **2006** School Center (under construction), Waidhofen/Ybbs (all Lower Austria). **In planning:** Hotel Training and Management Training Institute, Thimphu, Bhutan.

Steiner Sarnen Schweiz (SSS)
Pilatusstrasse 18
6060 Sarnen, Schweiz/Switzerland
www.steinersarnenschweiz.ch

Kommunikationsagentur, 1997 von **Otto Jolias Steiner** (geboren 1955 in Stans, Schweiz) in Sarnen (Zentralschweiz) gegründet. SSS entwirft, plant und realisiert Erlebniswelten, entweder als neugestaltete Projekte oder als Optimierung bestehender Anlagen; Spezialisierung auf Ausstellungen, Museen, Firmen- und Industriemuseen sowie Brandlands, Spektakel und touristische Destinationen; zahlreiche Vorträge und Auszeichnungen (u.a. Innovations-Anerkennungspreis 2003 der Zentralschweizer Handelskammer, 2005 Österreichischer Staatspreis für Tourismus, ‚Schönster Garten Italiens 2005' für die Gestaltung des Botanischen Gartens in Meran, ‚Besondere Sehenswürdigkeit der Region Stuttgart' für das Schreibermuseum in Stuttgart).

Projekte (Auswahl): **1993** Hergiswiller Glas Museum (Europäischer Museumspreis), Hergiswill, Schweiz **1998** Riedel Glas, Brandland, Kufstein, Tirol **2001** Schloss Neuenbürg, Regionalmuseum, Neuenbürg, Deutschland **2002** Expo.02 Schweizer Landesausstellung, Mechanisches Theater, Neuenburg, Schweiz; Swissarena, Verkehrshaus der Schweiz, Luzern, Schweiz **2003** LOISIUM Kellerwelt, Museum/Brandland, Langenlois, NÖ **2005** Glasmanufaktur Harzkristall, Brandland, Derenburg, Deutschland **2006** Glasmuseum Hentrich, Dauerausstellung, Düsseldorf, Deutschland; Zermattlantis, Matterhorn Museum, Dauerausstellung, Zermatt, Schweiz.

Communications agency founded in Sarnen, Central Switzerland, in 1997 by **Otto Jolias Steiner** (born in 1955 in Stans, Switzerland). SSS conceptualizes, plans and realizes *Erlebniswelten*, or 'worlds of experience,' either as original projects or as optimisations of existing facilities. SSS focuses on the design and realization of exhibits, public as well as company and industry museums, so-called 'Brandlands,' events and tourist destinations. Numerous lectures and awards, including the 2003 Recognition of Innovation Prize awarded by the Central Switzerland Chamber of Commerce; 2005 Austrian National Tourism Award for the LOISIUM project; the 'Most Beautiful Italian Garden of 2005' for the design of the Meran Botanical Gardens; the Stuttgart Schreiber Museum was honored as 'Most Notable Regional Place of Interest' in Stuttgart. Hergiswiller Glass Museum was recipient of the European Museum Prize.

Select Projects: 1993 Hergiswiller Glassworks, Hergiswill, Switzerland **1998** Riedel Glassworks Brandland, Kufstein, Tyrol **2001** Schloss Neuenbürg Regional Museum, Neuenbürg, Germany **2002** Expo.02 Swiss Regional Exhibition, Mechanical Theatre, Neuenburg, Switzerland; Swissarena, Swiss Transportation House, Lucerne, Switzerland **2003** LOISIUM Cellar World, Museum/Brandland, Langenlois, Lower Austria **2005** Harzkristall Glassworks Brandland, Derenburg, Germany **2006** Hentrich Glass Museum, permanent exhibit, Düsseldorf, Germany; Zermattlantis, Matterhorn Museum, permanent exhibit, Zermatt, Switzerland.

ko a la Landschaftsplanung
Gschwendter Strasse 81
8062 Kumberg, Österreich/Austria
www.koala.at

ko a la Landschaftsplanung (gegründet im Jahr 2000) arbeitet als interdisziplinäres Team in den Bereichen Freiraum- und Landschaftsplanung, Landschaftsarchitektur, Ökologie und Kunst.

Robert Kutscha geboren 1968 in Graz, Steiermark. Studium der Rechtswissenschaften in Graz und Gent, Studium der Landschaftsplanung in Wien, 1995 Europäische Kommission Brüssel, 1996–98 Wirtschaftskammer Steiermark, 1996–2001 Biobauer, 2002–2005 Vorstandsmitglied im Haus der Architektur Graz.

Veronika Oberwalder geboren 1967 in Lienz, Osttirol. Studium der Architektur in Graz, 1991–98 Mitarbeit und Projektleitungen in diversen Architekturbüros, 1998–2000 Management von Bewilligungsverfahren für Telecom-Sites.

Projekte (Auswahl): **2001** Innenhof GD Merkur Versicherung, Graz, Stmk. (Architektur Hans Illmaier) **2003** Grünanlagen Roche Diagnostics, Graz, Stmk. (Architektur Enst Giselbrecht) **2003** Außenanlagen Hypo Alpe Adria-Bank Klagenfurt, Ktn. (Architektur Thom Mayne) **2003** Außenanlagen Forschungsgebäude Biokatalyse der TU Graz, Stmk. (Architektur Ernst Giselbrecht) **2004** Außenanlagen Campus Fachhochschule Graz, Stmk. (Architektur Thomas Zinterl, Gonçalo Byrne) **2006** Außenanlagen Hotel und Besucherzentrum LOISIUM und Heurigenhof Bründlmayer, Langenlois, NÖ (Architektur Steven Holl).

In Planung: Gebäudebegrünung Wohn- und Geschäftshaus Marienmühle, Graz, Stmk. (Architektur Markus Pernthaler).

Founded in 2000, **ko a la Landscape Planning** works as an interdisciplinary team in the areas of recreational and landscape planning and architecture, ecology, and art.

Robert Kutscha born in 1968 in Graz, Styria. Studies in law in Graz and Ghent; studies in landscape planning in Vienna. 1995 European Commission, Brussels; 1996–1998 Styrian Chamber of Commerce. From 1996 to 2002, organic farmer. From 2002 to 2005, Chairman, Haus der Architektur in Graz.

Veronika Oberwalder born in 1967 in Lienz, East Tyrol. Studied architecture in Graz. From 1991 to 1998, project assistance and management at numerous architecture studios. 1998–2000 management of planning permission procedure for telecom projects.

Select Projects: 2001 Interior courtyard, GD Merkur Versicherung, Graz, Styria (architecture: Hans Illmaier) **2003** Green park zones, Roche Diagnostics, Graz, Styria (architecture: Ernst Giselbrecht) **2003** Outdoor complex, Hypo Alpe Adria Bank, Klagenfurt, Carinthia (architecture: Thom Mayne) **2003** Outdoor complex, Graz University of Technology Research Facility for Biocatalysis, Graz, Styria (architecture: Ernst Giselbrecht) **2004** Outdoor complex, University of Applied Sciences, Graz campus, Styria (architecture: Thomas Zinterl, Gonçalo Byrne) **2006** Outdoor complex, LOISIUM Hotel and Visitors' Center, Heurigenhof Bründlmayer, Langenlois (architecture: Steven Holl).

Projects in planning: Greening of Marienmühle residential and commercial building, Graz, Styria (architecture: Markus Pernthaler).

Othmar Pruckner geboren 1957 in Wien, aufgewachsen in Langenlois, NÖ. Lehramtsstudium Deutsch und Geographie, danach AHS-Lehrer; ab 1989 Journalist in *Falter*, AZ, *Der Standard*, *News*. Seit 2000 Redakteur im Wirtschaftsmagazin *trend*. Autor mehrerer Sach- und Reisebücher, darunter *Das Kamptal* (Wien, 1999) und *Das Waldviertel* (Wien, 2003). Österreichischer Preis für Reisejournalismus im Jahr 2000.

Dietmar Steiner geboren 1951. Studium der Architektur an der Akademie der bildenden Künste in Wien. Bis 1989 Lehrtätigkeit an der Hochschule für angewandte Kunst in Wien, an der Lehrkanzel für Geschichte und Theorie der Architektur. Seit 1993 ist Dietmar Steiner Direktor des Architekturzentrum Wien. 2002 kuratierte er als Kommissär den österreichischen Beitrag zur 8. Architekturbiennale in Venedig.
Er ist Mitglied des Advisory Committee des European Union Prize for Contemporary Architecture – Mies van der Rohe Award, der bedeutendsten europäischen Architekturauszeichnung – sowie Präsident von ICAM – International Confederation of Architectural Museums – der weltweiten Dachorganisation der Architekturmuseen. Als Architektur-Consultant für eine Vielzahl von Jurys und Gutachterverfahren tätig. Langjährige Redakteurs-tätigkeit beim italienischen Magazin *domus* sowie viele publizistische Arbeiten zu den Themen Architektur und Stadtentwicklung.

Gudrun Hausegger geboren 1962 in Graz. Studierte Medizin, Kunst- und Architekturgeschichte in Graz, Wien und Los Angeles. 1996–98 Presse- und Archivarbeit bei Coop Himmelb(l)au, 1998–2000 Lehrauftrag an der Universität für angewandte Kunst in Wien. Seit 1998 Mitarbeit im Architekturzentrum Wien. Publikationen im Rahmen von Coop Himmelb(l)au und dem Architekturzentrum Wien.

Othmar Pruckner born in 1957 in Vienna, grew-up in Langenlois/Lower Austria. Following training as a German and geography teacher, he taught at a secondary school; from 1989, worked as a journalist at *Falter*, AZ, *Der Standard*, *News*. Since 2000 editor of the business magazine *trend*. Has written numerous textbooks and travel books, including *Das Kamptal* (Vienna, 1999) and *Das Waldviertel* (Vienna, 2003). Austrian Prize for travel journalism in 2000.

Dietmar Steiner born in 1951. Studied architecture at the Academy of Fine Arts in Vienna. Until 1989 he held a teaching post in architecture history and theory at the College of Applied Arts in Vienna. Dietmar Steiner has been director of the Architekturzentrum Wien since 1993. In 2002 he curated the Austrian contribution to the Architecture Biennial in Venice in his capacity as Commissioner.
He is a member of the advisory committee for the European Union Prize for Contemporary Architecture—Mies van der Rohe Award, the most significant European architecture award, as well as being president of ICAM—International Confederation of Architectural Museums—the umbrella organisation for architecture museums world-wide. In addition, Dietmar Steiner works as an architecture consultant on a number of juries and for a number of appraisals. His many years' editorial experience with the Italian journal *domus* and many published articles on the topics of architecture and urban development are also among his activities.

Gudrun Hausegger born in 1962 in Graz. Read medicine, art history and architecture history in Graz, Vienna and Los Angeles. 1996–1998 press and archival work at Coop Himmelb(l)au, 1998–2000 teaching post at the University of Applied Arts in Vienna. Has been working at the Architekturzentrum Wien since 1998. Publications produced with Coop Himmelb(l)au and the Architekturzentrum Wien.